THE LEAPING HARE
NATURE
ALMANAC

Leaping Hare Press

First published in 2023 by Leaping Hare Press
an imprint of The Quarto Group.
One Triptych Place, London, SE1 9SH
United Kingdom
T (0)20 7700 6700
www.Quarto.com

A catalogue record for this book is available from the
British Library.

ISBN 978-0-7112-8538-5
Ebook ISBN 978-0-7112-8539-2

10 9 8 7 6 5 4 3 2 1

Designer **Hanri van Wyk**
Editorial **Nayima Ali, Elizabeth Clinton, Charlotte Frost,
 Kat Menhennet and Sofia Perdoni**
Illustrator **Raluca Spatacean**
Senior Commissioning Editor **Monica Perdoni**
Senior Production Manager **Maeve Healy**

Printed in China

THE LEAPING HARE

NATURE ALMANAC

Your Yearlong Mindful Guide
to Reconnecting with Nature

ILLUSTRATED BY
RALUCA SPATACEAN

CONTENTS

PEACE

WELLBEING

WISDOM

MINDFULNESS

CONNECTION

ECO-THERAPY

INTRODUCTION

Connecting to nature is part of who we are because that's what we are: nature.

When we are disconnected from the natural world, we are affected in many ways, physically, holistically and mentally. When the sun shines it lifts our mood, when we swim in the sea, we feel energised, when we feel a gust of fresh air it rejuvenates our spirits.

Immersing ourselves in nature from gardening to forest bathing reconnects us and reminds us of the therapeutic and wellbeing benefits that being out or around or aware and mindful of the natural world is well, the best thing ever.

The Leaping Hare Nature Almanac is a lush, big book for a mindful reason. It draws out the meaningful extracts rooted in our lovingly crafted titles that make our conscious-living list what it is, real and authentic, all in one organically, lush mindful mix.

Nature rituals; meditations; gardening; stargazing; visualizations and awareness are all practices we can incorporate into life every day. These earthy and eco-spiritual habits you will learn in this almanac will help ground you, nurture you and empower you to grow and flourish with nature by your side!

Structured around nature's seasons, this almanac explores each month of the year and shares insights into what we can do to honour, tune into and appreciate what nature gives us each and every day.

Like nature's cycles, our holistic health blooms, wilts and grows in life-affirming rhythms. Cultivating daily eco-spiritual habits empowers us all to thrive and nurture resilience simply by learning from nature's wisdom.

ME-YOU-NATURE. BE MINDFUL; BE HOPEFUL; BE LIFE!

ABOUT THIS BOOK

In this mindfully made almanac, each spread shares an insight into nature for the purpose of promoting connection, happiness, wellbeing and a sense of belonging all year round.

We encourage you to open this lovingly illustrated guide every day and unearth something enchanting about the natural world. Discover plant wisdom, lore and facts; learn how to connect holistically to nature through a meditation, ritual or recipe; or simply immerse yourself in the meditative joys of gardening.

Feel free to dip in and out, and letting the seasons guide you through nature's rhythms and our own too. Use the ribbon with intention to pick out the season or mindful month ahead.

Embrace the seasons, be empowered by nature's cycles and reconnect to the natural world.

WELLBEING

ECO-REFLECTION

WISDOM

GROWING

FORAGING

PLANT KNOWLEDGE

MEDITATION

STARGAZING

RECIPE

VISUALIZATION

RITUAL

JANUARY

*Time to reflect.
Rest, restore and look to the year
ahead with an open mind and spirit.*

NEW BEGINNINGS

Most of us experience dramatic upheavals in our lives – momentous points where we suddenly embark on a completely new path. This is often unexpected and painful – for example a divorce or losing a job – with all its attendant heartache and uprooting of possessions and routines. Alternatively, a new start may stem from an entirely positive choice. Many people make dramatic career changes by becoming self-employed or moving many miles to take on a new challenge.

Such moments do create a natural opportunity to pause and think about both the past and the future. This is the time to make fresh resolutions and to take new vows. The best of intentions can easily slip, but planting a tree can establish a living reminder to help keep you on the straight and narrow. As time dims the memory of the traumatic or challenging events that lie behind its planting, the steady growth and constant presence of the tree will serve as a constant aide-memoire.

INSPIRATION

The Anishinaabeg peoples from the Great Lakes revere the eastern white cedar. Its wood was whittled and bent to make the frames of their birch bark canoes, and its twigs were scattered on the fire to produce a fragrant smoke. This had a symbolic purifying role – a form of spiritual deep-cleanser.

CHOICE OF TREE

What better way to turn over a new leaf than to mark a change by planting a white cedar? Better still, it is well-suited to modern gardens. It is comparatively fast-growing, yet small (normally growing to no more than 60 ft/18 m). Despite this, at 1,350 years, cedars that grow in Southern Ontario are the oldest trees in Northeast America. In other words, it should long outlast even the most momentous change of direction yet remain a thing of permanent beauty. Neither you nor your heirs might be there to see it reach full maturity, but it is a concrete demonstration of faith in the new turn that life has taken.

PRACTICALITIES

Location is particularly important for such a private gesture. The tree should be planted in a secluded spot where you can retire to meditate quietly, away from intrusion. Also, unlike many ceremonial trees, this is a deeply personal living monument. It is a reminder to the individual, not to the world, thus no public explanation in the form of a plaque is needed. In some cases, however, it is appropriate to place a small label marked with the date and initials – a cryptic marker with which to intrigue a passerby in years to come.

NATURE AS RESTORER

Being out and about on our own can grant us the prospect of having quiet time without having to ask for it. Solo walks in the woods can help us drop into a more meditative state of connection with the land.

As we soak up the seasons, we are offered the opportunity to witness a perpetual progression taking place: the cycle of birth, death and rebirth that is reflected to us endlessly in the natural world, month after month, year after year. Although we almost take this perennial pattern for granted, it is an utterly key element of life, and it reminds us that creation, and re-creation, is the primary guiding principle on this planet. The organic matter that germinates, grows and decays back into the earth, also nourishes it.

PLANTS FOR WELLBEING

Having a living thing to care for teaches us responsibility. If we don't water it, prune it or expose it to light, then it may die. Taking care of the plant and appreciating how it is growing is mindful in itself: the process of looking after your plants can bring you straight into the present. Focus on the leaves, study the stems and veins and watch how they spread across the plant. Spray the plant, wipe down the leaves, nurture it, love it. The plant will be stronger, and the process will create a quiet, positive space in which to de-stress. Looking after plants is not as straightforward as it may seem. It takes time to know whether to water too much or too little, whether it will wilt or flourish near a heat source, and what level of light will suit it best. It's a skill that will be expressed in life itself: seeing a plant you've tended put out new leaves is a message from another living thing that you've paid attention. Spending a little time on plants can go a long way for wellbeing in the home.

Even if you live in a city-centre flat with a tiny balcony, you could plant tomatoes in the spring, herbs for year-round culinary use, or colourful flowers in pots to add interest to the space. If there is no outdoor space, you could use window boxes to grow and nurture plants and flowers. You can plant for the seasons, letting your flowers and herbs show you how time goes on.

Whatever your planting space, different seasons call for different kinds of cultivation, so it's a call to be in touch with the changes in weather and daylight. Each week you can plan a set time to take care of your plants, being alert to their changing needs. Whilst you're about it, if you have an outdoor space, you can incorporate planting that welcomes wildlife, connecting you even more with nature. The best herb varieties to encourage bees and butterflies are lavender, rosemary, thyme and sage; all hardy plants, low maintenance and easy to keep, whether in pots or in the ground.

BOÖTES

GREEK FOR: *plowman or herdsman*

The correct pronunciation for Boötes is bo-OH-tees, with the stress on the second syllable. The brightest star in the constellation is Arcturus (α Boötis), which is also the fourth brightest star in the night sky. In the 1790s, the French astronomer Jérôme Lalande stole a few stars from Boötes to create a new constellation, Quadrans Muralis ('the Quadrant') – named in recognition of his observatory's excellent equipment. However, Quadrans Muralis fell out of favour by the end of the nineteenth century and Boötes was returned to its original form. The name lives on, however, in the title of the early January Quadrantid meteor shower.

This constellation is home to the Boötes void. Cosmic voids are vast spaces between galaxies on the largest scale. The Boötes void, which was discovered in 1981 as part of a survey of galaxy distances, is approximately 700 million light years away and about 330 million light-years in diameter. It's one of the largest known voids in the Universe. If you were in a spaceship at the centre of the void you would see no stars in the sky with the naked eye.

CELESTIAL EVENTS

· January Quadrantids – *3 January*
  (originating from same parent-object
  of minor planet 2003 EH1 and Comet
  C/1490 Y1)
· June Bootids – *June 8–29* (originating
  from Comet 7P/Pons-Winnecke)

DEEP-SKY OBJECTS

· NGC 5466 – globular cluster

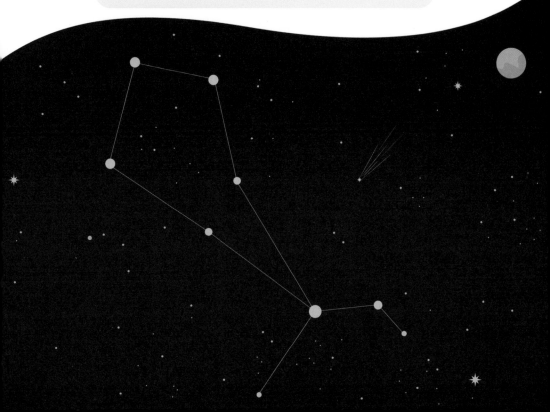

WATCH THE BIRDS MOVE

High up above, over rooftops and high-rises, down railway tracks, across grassy glades and the canopies of trees, the birds move, their choreography at odds with the pace on the streets below, our frantic human jazz. We can easily spot them; ascending the sky as if it possessed a steep rollercoaster, soaring, in swift flight, or simply drifting. Fleeing in cloudbursts, straggly lines, alone or in pairs – the city's birds move with grace, at complete ease with the air.

Watch as they move with the breath of the Earth, manoeuvring to the breeze, employing its force. Starlings migrate at night, when the air is calm and cool. Raptors seize on the currents rising up the sides of tall buildings to reach higher altitudes. Skeins of geese position wing tips in precisely the place to catch an upward gust, mastering aerodynamics to conserve energy in flight.

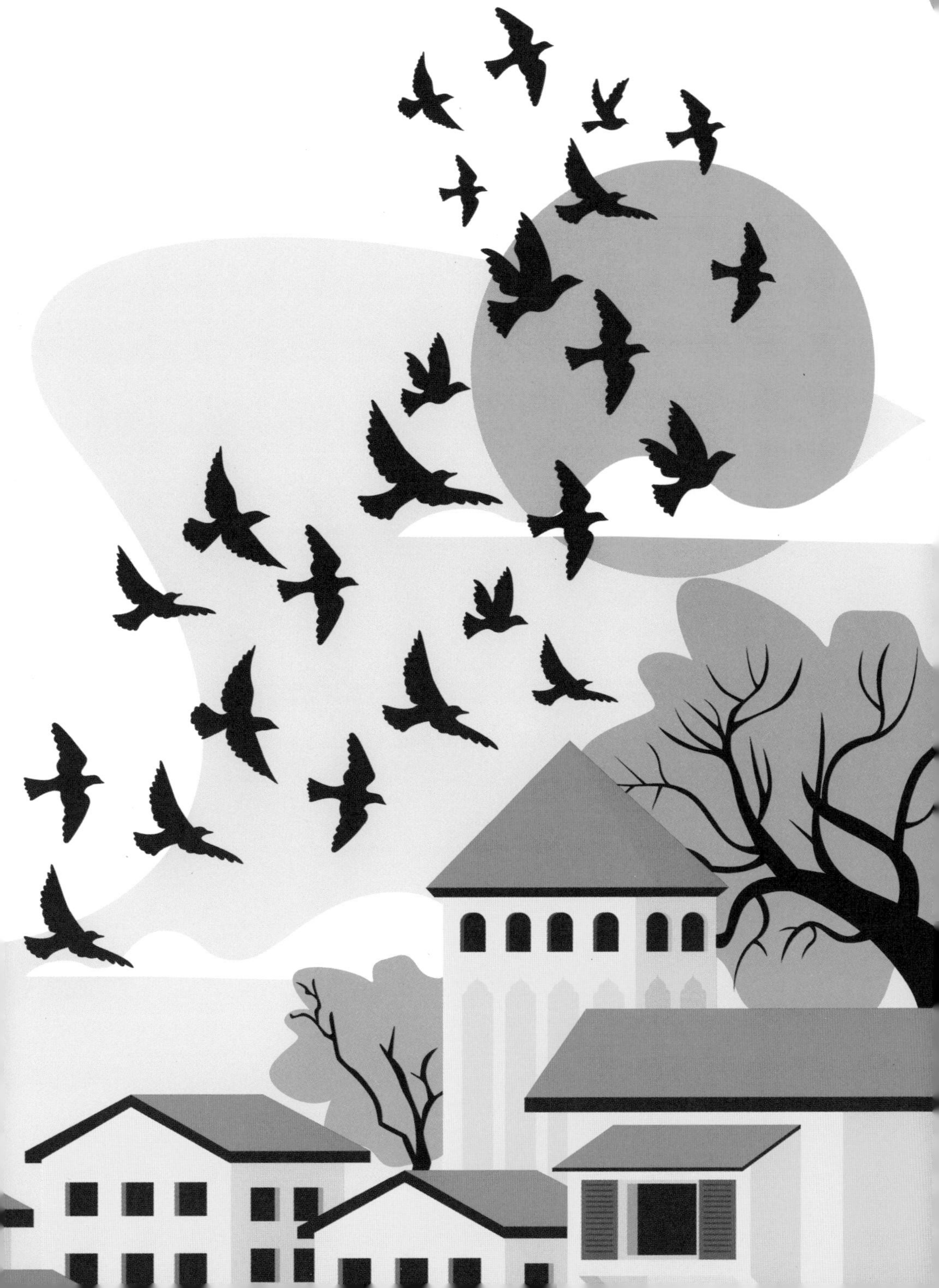

FOXES

Foxes have lived amongst us for centuries and they're celebrated in our folklore and myths. But whether the story is being told by the Greeks, Japanese, Celts, Native Americans, Disney or Roald Dahl, the fox is either portrayed as cunning, slippery and devious. Or, more favourably, as intelligent, adaptable and resourceful.

When the modern world transformed the fox's wild woods into avenues and office blocks, the fox, like any shrewd opportunist, saw a new world where the waste bins overflowed and the Saturday night streets were paved with castaway fast food.

It is incredible to believe that in our towns and cities these wild dogs live almost invisibly alongside us. If you're lucky you may see this relative of the wolf, dingo, jackal and coyote casually sauntering across your street, bringing a touch of the Serengeti to suburbia.

In January, foxes are at their most vocal. The spine-chilling scream of the vixen can sound like something from a horror film. This foxy lady is only fertile for a few days and her cry advertizes her availability, sparking bow-wows, barks and bickering from amorous dog foxes.

So now the festive season is over, if you've had enough of plastic snowmen and fake trees, take a short walk away from it all and step out into the darkness of the new year. Listen for your local foxes howling at the moon—the sound of survival. Let it stir something wild in your heart.

YOU ARE A PART OF THE NATURE YOU WALK THROUGH

Regular walkers are privileged in enjoying a view of the world denied to many people. Walking mindfully, we naturally learn to adjust our thinking about who we are as we stroll across our own small portion of the planet's surface, down country lanes, through city streets or out into the wild. We begin to recognize our links with nature, how we fit in to the web of life that surrounds us. We who walk upright, looking about us, appreciating beauty with thoughts full of questions, are as much products of the ecosystem as are the trees, bugs, butterflies or birds. It has taken humankind a long time to understand this.

TREES AT NIGHT

In the night we only see the silhouettes of trees, with beautiful highlights from the moon and the stars. They have the most amazing shapes, especially in the winter, when the branches are without leaves. Did you know trees sleep at night? Finnish researchers found that trees relax their branches in the evening, which they saw as a sign of snoozing. The researchers observed the branches and leaves of silver birches, which sagged as much as 10 cm/4 inches at night. They perked up again just before sunrise. The researchers concluded that because the branches lift up before the sun was up, the trees relied on their own internal circadian rhythm.

LOOK

Take an evening stroll and keep an eye out for the night trees. Look for a tree that speaks to you specifically. Are the leaves closed for the night? Do you see the branches sagging a little?

EUCALYPTUS
Eucalyptus globulus

There are around 300 species of eucalyptus, and this species is a very tall tree, able to reach heights of up to 100 m/300 ft at full spread.
It has pale bark, which tends to peel away, and the wood is aromatic.
The leaves are very pungent, usually slightly darker on the upper surface and pale beneath; they contain sacs filled with volatile oil.
The flowers are whitish, followed by round berries. Eucalyptus trees prefer hot climates but can be planted in temperate gardens provided the temperature does not fall below −5°C/23°F. They require well-drained soil and full sun. They will outcompete other plants and trees for water because they are experts at survival in their harsh native environment – the outback of Australia. In North Africa and southern Europe they have been deliberately planted in marshy areas to reclaim land and reduce the mosquito population.

Eucalyptus essential oil has been produced on a large commercial scale since the nineteenth century; it is commonly used in the pharmaceutical industry to make cold and cough remedies, and ointments for muscular aches.

PART OF PLANT USED Leaves

ACTIVE INGREDIENTS Volatile oil

COMMERCIALLY AVAILABLE AS Essential oil, cough medicine, lozenges, massage balm, ointment

ACTIONS Antiseptic, expectorant, vulnerary

USED TO TREAT

- · CUTS, GRAZES, WOUNDS: infusion of fresh leaves can be used to cleanse and disinfect affected areas; ointment can be applied as directed to speed healing.

- · SINUSITIS, COLDS: add two drops of essential oil to a bowl of boiling water and inhale the vapour for ten minutes to improve breathing; lozenges taken as directed also ease airways.

- · COUGHS: two drops of essential oil added to one teaspoon of sunflower oil massaged twice daily into the chest eases coughs; cough medicine can be taken as directed.

- · MUSCULAR ACHES AND PAINS: four drops of essential oil added to two teaspoons of sunflower oil massaged into affected areas twice daily eases pain and stiffness and improves movement; massage balm can be used as directed.

CULINARY USE None

SAFETY INFORMATION Infusion of fresh leaves or the essential oil should not be used on sensitive skin. Eucalyptus is toxic to animals.

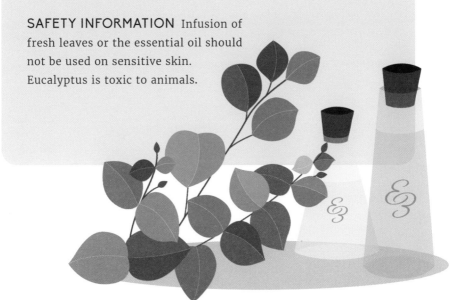

THE SUN ON YOUR BACK

There are still people alive today who can say 'When we were young, we looked at the sky to tell the time'. The position of the stars at night, or of the sun casting its shadows by day, was enough to fix the hour. Urban living, digital timepieces, watches and clocks have dulled this natural ability; we have become tied to the concept of precise time, for work, train and newscast. We have forgotten the sun.

Those of us who live in a temperate climate, where clouds and rain are frequent, are inclined to make comment, with surprise and pleasure, on a transitory burst of sunshine. The impermanent state of the weather is, for us, the norm and we have become accustomed to its changing patterns, even over the period of an afternoon's walk. So the sun breaking through clouds, warming our backs, can feel like a blessing and a gift, and we immediately feel grateful.

FEBRUARY

Time to be present. Seek out early morning naturescapes and reconnect to the wild beauty that exists.

TRULY IN NATURE

The bike connects us to the natural world almost as intimately as walking – with the added bonus that it enables us to see more of it in a given time. On the bike, we're part of the landscape, not merely passing through it; we have full use of senses we're deprived of in the car. We are truly in nature, not insulated from it. It's almost as though animals and birds understand that we pose no threat to them and therefore accept us into their world. And since our approach is silent, we can get much closer to them before they realize we're there.

NATURE'S REWARDS

For the mindful cyclist, being aware of wildlife is part of creating and maintaining a connection with the world and the seasons. Migrant birds tell me more surely than any calendar that the seasons are shifting: some arrive as harbingers of winter, whilst others bring summer with them from distant lands, and take it away again when they depart. We are privileged to share their space and freedom, breathe their air, feel their sun and rain and savour stolen glimpses of their hidden lives. They remind us that we are all part of the same living world, and finding our own way through it.

SMALL GARDENS

Sometimes we have to accept that we don't have the time or the space for a large garden. Rather than regard this as a failure or a deficiency, we can approach it as an opportunity to get creative. Gardens are about relationships – with plants, the Earth, our communities and ourselves. Any garden is a gift and a journey, even if it is one little pot of marigolds. The garden is what we make of it. The popularity of fairy gardens illustrates how a small garden can be just as rewarding and fun as a big plot of land.

Living in a small space doesn't just limit you to pots and hanging gardens, however. Consider other possibilities for spending time in the garden, such as community gardens, nearby gardens and school gardens. Volunteering at a local school garden, or tending an elderly neighbour's garden, is an opportunity for service and fitting in time with those good soil microbes and green brothers and sisters. Every plant, every plot of tended soil, makes the world a greener, fresher and more caring place. Every moment spent in a garden fills your heart with the compassion of green and growing things.

WALKING IN WET WEATHER

'Rain, rain, go away! Come again another day', chants the gloomy child at the window as the depressingly grey rain trickles down the glass, ruining dreams of football. The family who has planned a picnic looks anxiously up at the clouds; the organizers of an outdoor event check and recheck the weather forecast with fingers crossed. For those of us who live in places where rain is a regular but somewhat unpredictable feature of the climate, it is easy to fall into the habit of thinking of it as an irritation, a spoilsport. It is natural to do so. But the regular walker has a great opportunity to adopt a different attitude. We deepen our feelings for the world when we learn to relish the rain.

It is without doubt important to be prepared: dress sensibly and carry a waterproof when on a long hike. There is no sense in getting soaked to the skin unless a welcome hot shower is immediately available – and mindfulness is difficult to sustain when wet and shivering with cold. The aim of mindfulness is to see more clearly who we are and to understand our circumstances, to live more consciously and to dispel our inherited fog of ignorance. Cultivating a love for the rain gives us the opportunity to enhance our experience of living.

WHAT IS A LEAF?

A leaf can be defined as a vegetative outgrowth from the stem of a plant. The leaves of temperate-zone broad-leaved trees mostly have a flattened shape and are green in colour. However, that broad similarity encompasses a vast evolutionary diversity of form.

A leaf typically consists of the blade (lamina) and stalk (petiole). In the axil of the leaf, where the leaf joins the stem, there is an axillary bud. Some species also bear structures known as stipules. These are small and often leaflike, and are borne at the base of the leaf stalk. They are often small and inconspicuous, falling early, but sometimes they are large or useful for identification.

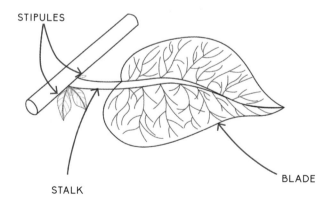

STIPULES

STALK

BLADE

TUNE INTO THE FOREST

One of the great benefits of birdwatching is not just the discovery of the birds themselves, but also of the environment around us; we see and experience it with new eyes and an enquiring wonder. When we look for birds in the forest, we are entering a new world, surrounded by some of the oldest living things on Earth. The primeval forests of the world are sadly shrinking through logging and careless agribusiness. Even so, there are still a great many forests, patches of deep woodland or wild scrub scattered about the globe. Forests are essential to the planet's health, breathing oxygen into the atmosphere and holding the soil together in times of flood; their biodiversity is rich and valuable.

MINDFUL BLOOMS

Fresh flowers evoke all sorts of emotions and make the house smell wonderful. Which rooms do you want to relax in? Would it be nice to wake up to the scent of flowers by your bedside, or would a few vases dotted around the home work better? The act of choosing the flowers can be a mindful experience; look at the shapes and textures of the leaves, the relaxing or stimulating colours of the petals, and the scent you might bring home – perhaps the powerful perfume of a lily, or the gentle aroma of a freesia.

Fresh flowers are a treat, but you could also have a bunch of dried herbs such as rosemary and thyme on hand to sniff as an everyday pick-me-up. Similarly, flowers are often used in essential oils; lavender is a popular choise to evoke calm and relaxation, and is one of the safer oils to use on bare skin. A few drops on your pillow at night or in a bathtub can become a wonderful element in your bedtime routine.

WHAT IS A SEED?

A seed contains an embryo (unborn plant), which is formed in the ovary of a flower. The embryo is surrounded by the cotyledon, which provides nutrition, and wrapped in the testa, a protective coat, which prevents the seed from drying out and protects it from any mechanical injuries that might occur after dispersal.

The sole purpose of a plant is to reproduce. There are male and female reproductive parts of the flower. Most flowers have both, but some flowers are single sex, such as pumpkin flowers. Some plants can reproduce vegetatively, by producing offsets and runners, but in most cases, seed production is the most effective way of ensuring the genetic diversity and long-term success of a species. Seeds are a food source to wildlife (and humans) and many of them won't reach germination. So, as an insurance, an individual plant can produce tens, hundreds and even thousands of seeds.

For a flowering plant to produce seeds it has to work in partnership with nature and adapt in ways that will attract partners such as insects, bees, butterflies, small mammals and birds. Insects help by transferring pollen from the anther (male) to the stigma (female), thus enabling fertilisation so that seeds can form in the ovary.

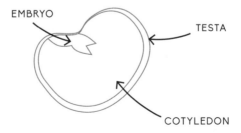

EMBRYO

TESTA

COTYLEDON

SEED SOWING RITUAL

Develop a deep well of patience and wisdom with this easy ritual.
If you have a garden, find a patch of soil and sit beside it. Alternatively,
you can use a plant pot filled with soil. You will also need some seeds of
your choice.

Close your eyes and take a few deep breaths. Imagine a beam of light
travelling down from the sky, hitting the top of your head and surging
through you.

Picture this light flowing into your hands and along your fingertips,
infusing you with creative energy. Open your eyes and dip the fingers of
both hands deep into the soil. Sift the earth rhythmically through your
fingers, as if you're adding air to this earthy mixture. As you do this
repeat the chant:

'I am at one with the universe and part of a much bigger picture.'

Sow the seeds, then cover lightly with the soil. To finish, water them, and
as you do this say:

'My patience grows, like the seeds I sow.'

The physical
activity of sowing and
then nurturing the seeds
also nurtures qualities within
yourself, like patience and
understanding. This, combined with a
powerful affirmation that is repeated
when the seeds are watered, helps
to reprogram the way you
think and feel.

MEDITATION

OBSERVE & LET IT FLOW

If your mind is a deep ocean, your thoughts are like fish and you are a deep-sea diver. Rather than noticing a fish and following it, try sitting cross-legged on the floor of the ocean and simply observe the fish as they swim by. In mindfulness, rather than trying to control a thought or following a thought and engaging with it, we just need to passively allow it to appear and move along. You can be certain that another thought will pop up just as quickly as the last one passed, but, with practice, they will not be as intense or engaging.

THE ELEMENTS

The earth, air, sun and water all have individual roles to play that help support, feed, hydrate, repopulate and produce food for a plant.

EARTH

Supports plants by allowing them to anchor their roots and communicate with one another. It also holds onto water and nutrients for plants to access when they need to.

AIR

Plants capture and absorb nutrients from the air, which are then transformed into food such as atmospheric water, carbon dioxide and nitrogen. The movement of air plays an important role in pollen and seed dispersal for some plants but can also cause damage and wind burn.

SUN

Plants have evolved throughout the world and adapted to different types of light. It is important to bear in mind a plant's origins so you can ensure you're providing it with the right light and temperature levels. Light varies in strength throughout the seasons, which tells plants when to start growing, fruiting and flowering, and when to hibernate. Sun also controls temperature, which affects all of the processes in a plant such as photosynthesis, germination and growth.

WATER

Plants are made up of 90% water and without it they become stressed and even die. Water hydrates plants and is used to dissolve soil minerals and deliver them to the plant. Plant cells fill with water, which is what keeps the stems strong and rigid. If the cells lose water the plant will wilt but can sometimes be resurrected by being watered again; but in extreme drought, a plant will perish. Too much water can also kill plants, by depriving them of oxygen from waterlogged soil.

SPRING

MARCH

APRIL

MAY

MARCH

*Time to be joyful. Spring brings
the promise of freedom, new
growth and fresh experiences.*

ECO-REFLECTION

FREE SPIRITS

It is not uncommon for us to dream of flying. Free from the tug of gravity we glide down a hillside or across the landscape, feet no longer engaging with the Earth; a half-lost memory of liberation lingers when we wake. Birds are the free spirits of the natural world – agile, aerial inhabitants of the rich environment we all share. Much of their attraction lies in the way they come and go in their own time, unhindered by fences, unrestrained by weight. Deep down, we envy their ability to fly.

Birds do not belong to a particular place, though they have their own wide territories. The birds that we feed do not belong to our garden, although we may see them there regularly and talk easily of 'our goldfinches' or 'our hummingbirds'. We may even come to recognize some individuals: the friendly bird that watches as we dig the garden or becomes very interested in the compost we spread around the roses. But open the garden door and the birds on the feeder are off in a flash, disappearing into bushes or over the hedge and away. They take flight and vanish. The same rapid dispersion happens when a hawk casts its sinister shadow cruising low through the garden on the hunt for a meal.

AURIGA

LATIN FOR: *charioteer*

Auriga is part of the Perseus group of constellations that are connected to the Perseus myth. It is known as 'the Charioteer' and was so named because its brightest stars (including Capella and Menkalinan) formed a shape that reminded the Romans of the pointed helmet of a charioteer.

Auriga is the site of the Galactic Anticentre, the point in the sky directly opposite the Galactic Centre as viewed from Earth. The Galactic Centre is the centre of our Milky Way galaxy (located in the constellation Sagittarius). Because it is located on the band of the Milky Way, Auriga has many bright open clusters within its borders that are easy targets for amateur telescopes. It also hosts Capella (α Aurigae), the sixth-brightest star in the night sky.

BEST TIME TO OBSERVE

Auriga calls to mind the shepherds who stay with their flocks on the hillside for months at a time, living in tune with nature and the seasons, and likely very knowledgeable about the night sky. The life of a shepherd must be tough and often lonely, but their job is simple – take care of the flock. Today, many of us crave a life more like this: simpler, in contact with nature, and time to just sit and be. When life gets busy it's often these simple things that we cut out first. But when we stop doing things that nourish us, we become depleted and stressed. Auriga can remind us to be more shepherd-like – simplify things, take time and notice the rhythms of life.

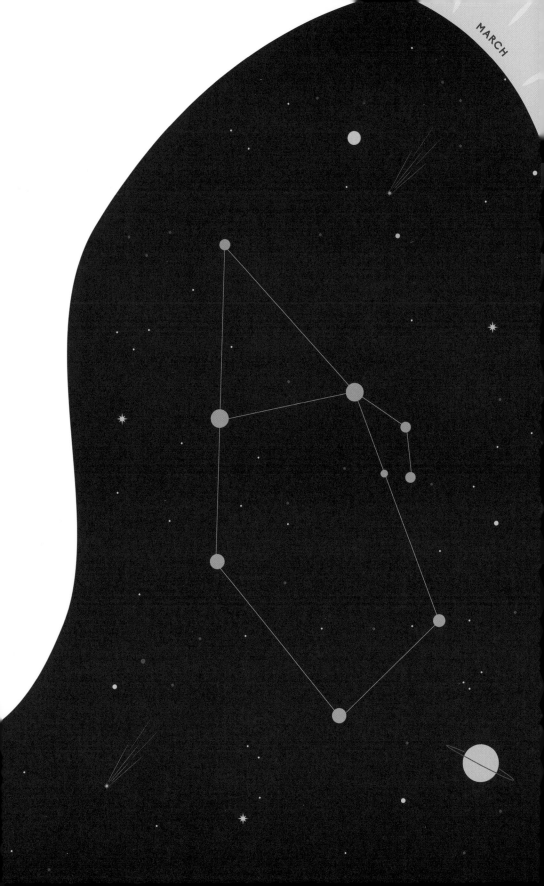

GARDENING

Gardening is more than just a functional activity. If human beings needed only nutrition, they wouldn't grow flowers or put benches in their gardens. Gardening nourishes our minds as well as our bodies—it is part physical workout, part therapy and meditation. It also reconnects us with nature and tops up our vitamin D. So while many community gardens are simply a way of combining food production with socializing with your friends, some use the many gifts that gardening offers to help educate, inspire, and heal.

Why does gardening feel so good? It is repetitive but challenging. You can let your mind wander while weeding. You get exercise and fresh air, which is vital for the health of a society leading increasingly sedentary lives. On a social level, gardening can take you away from people if you need peace and quiet. Conversely, many of us began searching for connection after the isolation of Covid lockdowns, in this case gardening can offer a nonthreatening environment in which to find this. Whatever your skill level or social confidence, there is something there for you.

WHAT IS A TREE?

We all recognize a tree when we see one, and there are plenty of characteristics that allow us to distinguish an oak from a beech, or an apple tree from a pear tree. But it is surprisingly difficult to pin down the defining characteristics of trees in general.

When trying to define a tree, we can begin by saying that it is a perennial (that is, long-lived), woody plant with normally a single, defined stem that reaches at least 3 or 4 m/10 or 13 ft tall. This feature usually distinguishes it from a shrub (also a woody perennial), which has several to many stems from the base, and is shorter. However, there is no clear distinction between trees and shrubs at the point at which they meet. A tree can have more than one stem, and sometimes several. Moreover, many species can grow as either a shrub or a tree. For example, many trees, whilst they make magnificent specimens in the lowlands, will be reduced to stunted shrubs when growing on mountains or in other exposed positions.

RECYCLING IN THE GARDEN

Repurposing is ecological – reuse reduces waste – and economic. It feels creative and resourceful, like throwing together a meal from the last of the leftover ingredients.

Gardens lend themselves to repurposing and reusing. Whether it's a plant from a neighbour, a gate of wooden pallets or a chicken coop of scrap wood, recycling turns the garden into an ever-evolving masterpiece of innovation. As you spend more time in a garden, you get to know it better, from the way light hits different areas throughout the changing seasons to where certain soils can be found. Friends and resources show up, then move on to greener pastures. One year you decide to plant a pear tree, another time you contemplate adding chickens. Children come and go, and the pear tree gets bigger. The garden is a long conversation between the land and the gardener.

NATURE AS A SANCTUARY

Creating an indoor garden is not a major undertaking, but the addition of attractive houseplants can bring a new source of pleasure into the home. Over time, you can see the changes as your plants grow and develop new leaves and blooms. You could even propagate new shoots and give the baby plants to friends and family. (Although do bear in mind that certain plants are poisonous to humans or animals, and keep them well out of reach if this might be the case. Plants, like every other living thing, need to be treated with respect.)

When you feel like things are getting on top of you in life, nurturing plants can help you get back in control. Whilst you will never be able to fully have your life in order, you can decide how to arrange your plants, what vegetables you want to grow, where the pot plants can move to, and how frequently you feed and water them. Bad day at work? Spend some time looking after your indoor plants, wiping off the dust and checking they are not too dry. Outside, cut back the deadheads, turn over the soil and pull up the weeds, leaving a clean canvas for your other plants to thrive. The act of caretaking is healing in itself: by handling your plants with gentleness and skill, care and attention, you are literally growing yourself a better living environment. You do it for them and for you at the same time, experiencing a balance between being the one who cares and the one who is cared for. Look after your botanical friends, and let them cheer you up.

CARROTS
Daucus carota subsp. sativus

Easy to grow, although not necessarily easy to grow well, carrots are a staple of most vegetable plots and community gardens. Quick-maturing cultivars can produce early crops, especially if grown under cover, whilst later cultivars, stored well, can last through much of the winter.

PLANTING TIPS

To an extent, sowing density depends on cultivar, soil type and how big you want your carrots. You could sow a little more than needed and thin to the desired spacing, although some believe this can attract pests by bruising the leaves and releasing the carrot smell.

CULTIVATION

Small amounts of seed can be sown every few weeks to avoid a bumper crop later in the season and to ensure continuity of supply. Whilst it is useful to water carrots during dry spells, they should not be overwatered. If you can, leave a few plants to go to seed, because carrot flowers and seeds are particularly good for attracting beneficial insects.

WEED CONTROL

Carrots need a lot of weeding to avoid being swamped, especially in wet years. Try this trick to give you a head start: sow the seeds and then cover the end of the row with a sheet of clear plastic. The weeds under the plastic will germinate a little quicker. As soon as you see weeds showing under the plastic, go over the whole row with a weed burner. This will kill all weeds that have germinated in the rest of the row but that are not yet showing. The carrots themselves will not be harmed, because they germinate a little slower.

HARVEST

The roots can be harvested at any size, although they are awkward to handle when small. Roots left in the ground too long may experience pest damage. You can also eat the foliage, which can be added to soups and stews. The seeds are also edible.

CONTAINER TIP

Carrots also grow well in containers. Try to find short, early, or quick-maturing cultivars and water well.

LIFESPAN Two or three seasons

PLANT Sow directly into soil or containers from spring onward but not when temperatures go above 29°C/85°F

GROW IN Best in a light, sandy soil, but adequate crops can be grown in most situations

WILD SCENTS OF NATURE

You walk through woodland in the spring, perhaps along a winding path made by a badger, when suddenly you catch the scent of garlic – wild garlic. You stop and look about you and there, beneath the bushes and around the fallen timber and old decaying tree stumps, white flowers are bursting from a carpet of fresh, glossy green leaves. You have caught the scent and you breathe it in. Savour it: the wild scents of nature are elusive; we have forgotten how to enjoy them.

With sensory awareness, the world is revealed in a new light. The landscape is no longer something that we are just passing through and observing; we feel organically part of our world, fully immersed and present. The way that we experience the landscape and plant life through our senses reminds us too that we are a holistic and integral part of nature.

WHAT IS A SEEDBOMB?

Firstly, they are not explosive or edible! A seedbomb is a little ball made up of a combination of compost, clay and seeds.

WHAT IS IT FOR?

The compost and clay act as a carrier for the seeds so they can be launched over walls or fences and into inaccessible areas such as wasteland or railways.

BUT WHAT IS THE POINT? WHY CAN'T YOU JUST THROW SEEDS LOOSE?

Most seeds are very light and there is risk of them being blown away by the wind, making them unsuitable for launching long distances.

HOW DO I MAKE THEM?

There are various ways of making seedbombs. You need to find a carrier for the seeds. This method uses natural ingredients – compost and clay. The compost offers nutrients for the seeds to germinate and grow strong during their infancy, and the clay binds the seedbomb, making it hard enough not to break when it hits the ground.

HOW DO THEY WORK?

After about three weeks, the first seedlings work their way through the seedbomb and root into the ground below. The seedlings will then grow into mature plants and face whatever conditions Mother Nature has in store for them. As they grow, more seeds germinate and the seedbomb begins to dissolve. This can take days, weeks or months – it depends on the quantity of rainfall. Seeds will remain dormant until their environmental needs are met with these factors: water, correct temperature and a good position to grow in. There is a sense of unpredictability with seedbombing. Its random nature is what attracts people; the magic of waiting to see if this strange little ball will spring to life … if it actually works.

AIR

Nature can move us physically and emotionally, and there are few better ways to experience that than enjoying how the air can buffet us about. Go out in wild winds and let yourself be blown about and hold your jacket out like a parachute; fly kites and watch them soar high in the sky; try windsurfing and feel the air drive you across the water; watch the air flows catch the sparks from your bonfire and send swirling smoke into the sky. This is nature acting directly upon you.

*Allow the air to flow
through your inner self.*

*Connect to nature's
breath and become
one with the wind.*

Be wild; be free; be you.

Let your spirit soar.

APRIL

*Time to be still. Notice and observe
the stars, seas and magical
skies in all of nature's hues.*

THE USEFULNESS OF WEEDS

The kinds of weeds present in a garden or other habitat can tell us about the land itself, as well as what minerals may be present or lacking. Foxtail, horsetail and willow indicate that the land will be wet and swampy, during at least part of the year. Chicory and bindweed indicate compacted soil. Dandelions, mullein, yarrow and nettles indicate an acidic soil, whilst field pepperwort and campion show you the soil is alkaline. Gardeners can use these indicators to tell us either what will grow well in this soil, or what remediation is needed. One reason these weeds grow in their particular soil conditions is simply that they can, but another is that they offer some remediation to the soil's challenges.

Bindweed and clover work to break up soil. Dandelions and sunflowers accumulate minerals in their plant tissue, which can either help pull minerals from deep down and make them available to surface-growing plants, or actually remove excess minerals from the soil. This is so effective it is used to remediate toxic soil. Here we again see an example of the dynamic relationship between soil and plants. We are reminded that plants aren't just growing things, but have a purpose in a web we only slightly understand.

We can benefit from these weeds' gifts directly as well. Dandelions, when one eats the whole of the plant, provide a complete protein. They are highly nutritious and, since they are so easy to grow, could help to provide a solution to malnutrition in some parts of the world. Learning how to eat the weeds in your garden cultivates a whole new relationship with the land.

RECIPE

JAPANESE KNOTWEED PRESERVE

This rebel was introduced into Europe from Japan in the mid-nineteenth century and soon became the gardener's new best friend as it was large, ornamental and grew like crazy. Gardeners soon lost control and it became their worst enemy, as it land grabbed all available space. A word of warning: it is now deterred and you can be prosecuted for allowing it to spread into the wild.

UPSIDE There's plenty of it, and it's easy to get at.

WHERE TO FIND IT Temperate ecosystems – roadsides, wasteland.

WHAT'S GOOD ABOUT IT? It's edible, looks like the lovechild of asparagus and bamboo and tastes like rhubarb, although on the sour side. Some people call it donkey rhubarb or salty rhubarb.

GETTING IT EDIBLE Peel off fibrous outer skin and discard, then soak stems in water for 12 hours before making your recipe.

INGREDIENTS

- 2 kg/4 lbs Japanese knotweed – ideally harvested in spring or early summer - leaves discarded
- 2 tbsp cardamom pods
- 1.2 kg/2 lbs unrefined caster sugar
- Juice of 1 lemon

METHOD

1. To prepare your knotweed, discard the leaves and soak the stems in water for 12 hours before cooking.

2. Toast the cardamom pods in a small skillet over a medium heat until they start to pop and go light brown. Be careful as they can be quite lively. Then take the pan off the stove and leave to cool.

3. Once cool, grind the pods quite finely in an electric spice grinder or pestle and mortar until the seeds inside are completely ground. If using a pestle and mortar, you will need to sieve out the skins of the pods as they won't break down with the pestle.

4. Mix the ground cardamom with sugar and leave for 24 hours to infuse.

5. Once you are ready to make the preserve, wash the knotweed stems and chop them roughly into 5-cm/2-inches pieces.

6. Place the knotweed stems into a heavy based pan with 1 cup of water and place on a medium heat. Once the knotweed chunks have started breaking down, slowly add the cardamom sugar and lemon juice. Stir to combine. Bring the preserve to the boil and cook until setting point (105°C/220°F).

7. Take the pan off the stove and leave to rest for five minutes, stirring to distribute any bubbles, which will slowly disappear.

8. Pour the preserve into warm sterilized jars (make sure you sterilize your lids too) and leave it to set with the lid on.

CHANGING ATTITUDES

Ultimately we need to accept the weather as it is. We may not particularly like being wet or cold but we can take physical interventions to insulate ourselves from the worst of it. The important difference is the spirit with which we approach facing the elements: do we grit our teeth and fight our way against the wind and rain, shoulders tight and head down?

Accepting the weather and heading out, appropriately attired, with a positive attitude, we may find there is more pleasure to be gained than we expected. When we live in the moment we can challenge the negative thinking and feel liberated and exhilarated. One moment the wind in your face may be hard to battle against and the rain is a strength-sapping drenching. At these moments focus on maintaining your form, accept the slower pace but keep moving. Seeing it as a battle is never going to work; fighting the wind will not make it stop blowing. However, at some point you will turn a corner and suddenly the wind is your friend – like a hand in the small of your back the wind urges you onwards, encouraging you towards your goal, and as you warm up, the rain becomes refreshing, a pleasantly cooling drizzle.

Sometimes the combination of the elements can be so bad as to be laughable – freezing rain with horizontal winds driving it into your face like shards of glass, making forward motion almost impossible.

URBAN GARDENING

Thriving urban gardens are rebellious little things. Whether it's a window box stuffed with herbs or a teeny backyard hosting a jungle of luscious plants, leaves as large as frying pans, there's someone behind the creation of each, determined to bring beauty to a space, no matter how small. What makes them equally cheering sights is that they have often been planted to delight not just the gardener themselves, but their neighbourhoods and communities too. City gardeners, from Tokyo to Los Angeles, often have socially focused motivations that drive the desire to plug a few plants into a scrap of compost.

A scatter of pots or a couple of hanging baskets can change our experience of the city, from one of tyres and bricks to one of scent, colour and texture. They also make a statement about how you want the city to be. Little gardens can indicate that the person or community who made them wish to live in a city that has clean air and supports pollinators and sustainable ecosystems. Even the tiniest verdant patches create a purifying tonic for the surrounding environment; they purify the air, as plants remove carbon dioxide and pump out oxygen, and provide scraps of soil that absorb rainfall run-off from impervious roofs and streets. They are also rich seams of nectar and pollen. Bees, birds, beetles, bats, butterflies and moths are suffering dangerous declines all over the globe due to feeding and nesting habitat loss, misuse of chemicals and changes in climate patterns – making islands of flowers, in private or public spaces, ever more vital. Raising these gardens in a limited space has many rewards for the generous grower. When pollinators fertilize your plants, they turn your garden from a collection of buds to a flourishing success – kick-starting reproduction, setting seed for the next season and even ensuring delicious food crops for your dinner plate.

WHITTLE A PLANT LABEL

A plant label is a useful thing. As the seasons change, it provides a reminder of what has been planted where. It can be invaluable in a complex garden or when looking after germinating seeds. This example is made from chestnut, which is high in tannins and will rot less readily. Oak would be another good option; other woods will work fine but may rot more quickly. You can make plant labels in many different shapes, but a simple design like this one is particularly good when making multiple labels. The simplest option is to write the plant name onto the label with a pencil, but pencil often wears off over time. For something more permanent, you can carve the letters using the tip of your knife or, as here, make a tool (akin to an awl) to impress the letters using a kind of dot font. Slowly count to three whilst peeling a shaving, as this can help you be present.

MAKES 1

TOOLS & MATERIALS

- Rectangular billet, such as chestnut or oak, for the plant label
- Slöjd knife
- Short length of hazel for the awl
- Crosscut saw
- Clamp or bench hook
- Drill
- Drill bit to match
- Nail diameter
- Nail
- Metal file
- PVA glue (optional)

METHOD

1. Using the Slöjd knife, remove any bark and sapwood from the billet. The sapwood has a paler tone and is the wood closest to the bark. It needs to be removed because it is more prone to rotting.

2. Take a shaving off all the other surfaces to clean up the wood into a rectangular cross-section. Be sure to remove the pith before thinning the wood to the desired thickness. Aim for a nice smooth surface; this will shed rain more easily and provide a clean surface to write on.

3. Carve a point at one end of the label, where it will be pushed into the ground.

4. Chamfer all the edges of the label, especially the point that will be pushed into the ground. This will make it stronger.

5. Carve a rectangular bevel on the non-pointed end of the label.

6. To make the awl, saw a short length of hazel to form the handle, using a clamp or bench hook to hold the hazel in place.

7. Drill a hole into the end of the handle for inserting a nail. Choose a drill bit of a suitable size for the nail; the aim is to achieve a snug fit. For best safety, the wood should be clamped for drilling.

8. File off the head of the nail and insert it into the drilled hole. When the hazel dries, it will hold the nail tight. If you are using very dry wood, use PVA glue to fix the nail in place.

9. Mark the letters onto the plant label in pencil, then push the point of the awl into the wood, spacing the dots evenly along the lines of the letters.

TREES ARE FAMILY

Applying a touch of humanity to one square metre of the city can be a powerful action that is both fulfilling and beneficial for your neighbourhood. Adopting a street tree is one example. Take a newly planted sapling that's recently appeared near your home or workplace. Water it occasionally, loosen the straps that tether it to its stakes as it gains strength as a service to horticulture – but also to ensure the enduring wellbeing of your metropolis. As the sapling's trunk matures from a skinny whip to a burly adult that can hold its own in a harsh, competitive environment, imagine the many city dwellers who will be able to take respite under the shade of its lush awning on a sweltering day, and enjoy the chance to inhale the pocket of fresh air the plant has gifted to them.

Somehow, trees make us inhale more deeply than anywhere else. It is as if the body instinctively responds to the oxygen shrouded about them. Trees, those grand masters of air purification, help us to feel safer letting our lungs expand to their max. Breathing deeply like this is a pick-me-up that feels as refreshing as a dip in the ocean. But it is crucial to remember that breathing well is so intrinsic to our state of mind that it's important to find times – and places – where we can regularly enjoy the restorative act of inhaling and exhaling. The shallow, high chest breathing we adopt whilst running between meetings, hunched over a desk or waiting for that delayed train keeps our hearts ticking. But it doesn't feed our bodies, or our minds for that matter, with the full health benefits of a deep, relaxed abdominal inhalation.

THE ANATOMY OF LEAVES

The structure of leaves is closely linked to their function. Leaves need to absorb light, conserve water and take in and release gases in order to photosynthesize. The epidermis of their upper and lower surfaces is usually one cell thick, which protects the leaf's internal tissues, prevents water loss, and bears other structures such as the stomata and any hairs or scales. It is translucent to allow light through, and is covered with a waxy cuticle that is usually thicker on the upper surface and defends against water loss. Stomata are small pores formed by guard cells on the surface of a leaf that can expand or contract to open or close, controlling the passage of gases. Unlike most of the epidermis, the guard cells contain chloroplasts. Most stomata are present on the lower leaf surface where they are protected from the drying effects of the sun.

INSIDE THE LEAF

The tissue between the two layers of epidermis (the 'mesophyll') is formed of two layers in dicotyledonous plants. Just below the upper epidermis is the palisade mesophyll. These cells, which are closest to the light, contain the most chloroplasts necessary for photosynthesis. The chloroplasts can be damaged by excessive radiation so they move within the cell depending on how much light there is.

The part between the palisade mesophyll and the lower epidermis is known as the spongy mesophyll. This comprises loosely packed, rounded cells, which contain fewer chloroplasts than those of the palisade parenchyma but are still able to photosynthesize. The leaf veins pass through the layers of the mesophyll, transporting water and minerals around the leaf and products of photosynthesis, such as glucose, to other parts of the plant. They also have associated thickened cells that support the leaf.

LEAF STALKS

Leaves may have a stalk (petiole) or not, in which case they are described as sessile. The conducting tissues of the leaf midrib or veins pass to the stem of the plant through the petiole, if present. The petiole serves to support the leaf and to transport water and nutrients to and from the rest of the plant.

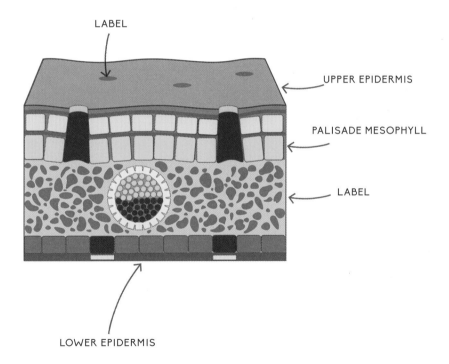

LABEL

UPPER EPIDERMIS

PALISADE MESOPHYLL

LABEL

LOWER EPIDERMIS

CELESTIAL GARDENING

Ever since our ancestors first poked a seed in the ground, the skies above them have influenced their approach to gardening and men and women have used the regular cycles of the skies as a calendar. They observed that crops grew better when planted at certain times.

As the years passed, ancient civilizations discovered the brightest stars were planets and gave each a zodiac sign. The monthly path of the moon passed through these planets, and the moon and the planets became intertwined as a gardening guide. Certain tasks are assigned to certain planets when the moon passes them.

MOON PATHS

For two weeks of each month, the moon 'ascends' (climbs higher) in the sky and the next two weeks it descends closer to the horizon. During the moon's ascent and descent it passes through star constellations, which affect earthbound elements like the rise and fall of sap.

CONSTELLATIONS

During the lunar cycle, the moon spends about two days in each zodiac sign. The zodiac signs are further categorized by elemental signs such as earth, air, fire and water, which has a beneficial 'action' on the plant: for example, water signs channel energy into leaf growth and leafy plants such as lettuce and spinach.

Celestial gardening is a mystifying practice but something that is intriguing enough to incorporate into your garden, even if it is a small test bed in the corner. The outcome could be surprising!

The days the moon passes through the zodiac signs have aptly been named:

FRUIT DAYS – FIRE SIGNS (*Aries, Leo, Sagittarius*)
Plant all fruit on these days, such as strawberries, blueberries, plums, apples; and fruiting vegetables, such as beans, tomatoes and squash; as well as crops grown for their edible seeds, such as sunflowers and cereals.

FLOWER DAYS – AIR SIGNS (*Gemini, Libra, Aquarius*)
Plant beautiful, fragrant, ornamental flowering plants and edible flowers, such as nasturtiums.

ROOT DAYS – EARTH SIGNS (*Taurus, Virgo, Capricorn*)
Plant edible roots, such as carrots and radishes, as plants will produce strong anchoring roots at this time.

LEAF DAYS – WATER SIGNS (*Cancer, Scorpio, Pisces*)
Leafy plants – such as lettuce, spinach and brassicas, and fruits with high water content, such as cucumber – will thrive if planted on leaf days.

A PEACEFUL SPACE

Bathing allows us to bring full awareness to our body, checking in with every part of ourselves both physically and mentally. Washing gives us an opportunity to take care of our physical vessels, to clean away any dirt and bacteria along with our troubles and anxieties.

A mindful bathroom can be created with nature in mind, using greenery to incorporate the outdoors within your four walls, as well as oxygenating the air. A good bathroom is efficient, of course, but it can also be set up for enjoyment, a meditative space for rest and rejuvenation. For those wondering how best to create a verdant space, air plants, bamboo and succulents are commonly used in bathrooms to withstand the steam from hot showers and water. Work with the nature of the plants, and they'll reward you. A peace and quiet bath allows us to slow down to an absolute stop, allowing ourselves to have space to think, to not think, or simply be present with our calming surroundings. Parents can relish the solitude of the bathroom once children are asleep, the soothing noises and scents calming the senses after a hectic day. It's like pushing the reset button, whether you have a shower to wake up or a bath to relax and create calm. We emerge as a new and fresher version of ourselves.

APRIL

GROWING

DAISY
Bellis perennis

This is the humble little white flower with a golden centre that loves to grow in green grass – the common daisy. Whilst perfectionist gardeners would rather eradicate it with weed killer, it might pay to keep it – the flowers have medicinal properties that have been long forgotten. One example is their soothing effect on bruises, which is somewhat similar to arnica though much milder.

Daisies are perennial, with flowers that open at daybreak and track the sun through changing warmth and daylight – hence the name daisy, from the Old English 'day's eye'. In the past, the daisy was valued as an herbal remedy because of its easy availability. As a first-aid treatment for bruises and wounds, or a soothing cough medicine, it played an important part in daily life and was recorded in many old herbal documents as a folk medicine.

If you want to use daisies for making herbal preparations such as ointment or macerated oil, pick the flowers and use them fresh on the day, as they wilt quickly.

PART OF PLANT USED Flower heads

ACTIVE INGREDIENTS Bitters, flavonoids, mucilage, tannins, volatile oil

COMMERCIALLY AVAILABLE AS Not used in commercial preparations

ACTIONS Astringent, expectorant, vulnerary, anti-inflammatory

USED TO TREAT

- WOUNDS, CUTS, GRAZES: an infusion of fresh flowers, cooled, and applied to injured areas soothes pain, cleanses dirt, and encourages wound healing.
- BRUISES: macerated oil or ointment made with fresh daisy flowers applied gently 2–3 times daily soothes pain and inflammation.
- SPOTS, ACNE: an infusion of fresh flowers, cooled, makes a soothing and antiseptic skin wash.
- COUGHS: an infusion of fresh flowers with a teaspoon of honey added, taken 2–3 times daily, soothes a tickly cough.
- INDIGESTION, POOR LIVER FUNCTION: Indigestion, poor liver function: an infusion of the fresh flowers taken 2–3 times daily eases cramps and supports the liver to digest oily foods.

CULINARY USE Young leaves taste a bit like spinach and can be added to green salads

SAFETY INFORMATION No issues

MAY

*Time to be free. Seashores, sand
and wind are nature's gifts.*

CREATING YOUR OWN HERB GARDEN

Designing a herb garden is a lovely, creative task. It pays to think about what kind of herbs you want to grow and how you want to use them. Consider how much space you have and how you will lay out your herbs.

A SIMPLE HERB GARDEN LAYOUT

One of the easiest herb gardens to create is a 3 m/10 ft square, marked by a border of stones or bricks. Lay paving stones in a checkerboard pattern within the square, leaving bare squares of soil in between. Plant different herbs in each soil space; the paving stones let you step between them for easy picking.

PLANNING A HERB GARDEN

Creating a useful garden that is relevant to you means you will be out in it all the time and interacting with your plants regularly.

- If you want to use fresh herbs in cooking, and also to dry or preserve some for the winter months, consider herbs such as rosemary, basil, thyme, tarragon, fennel, marjoram, sage and garlic.
- If you want to grow herbs to use for general health, to make teas and other preparations, then consider feverfew, Lady's mantle, Roman camomile and echinacea.
- If you want to use herbs for something more specific, such as taking care of your skin, then consider the following: lavender, red clover, Roman camomile, myrtle and calendula.

If your garden is already established, the herbs will need to fit into its existing layout. Check where there is room to plant your herbs, and whether the spaces are in light or shade, as this will influence the plants you might choose.

If you are starting a herb garden from scratch, then find the sunniest, warmest, and most sheltered part of your garden, because most culinary and medicinal herbs will thrive there.

HERB PLANTING

HERB CHOICES FOR FULL SUN

Dill, tarragon, fennel, hyssop, bay, lavender, oregano, cilantro, basil, sweet marjoram, rosemary, sage and myrtle.

These Mediterranean aromatic herbs have special cells within their leaves that contain volatile oils – highly concentrated fragrances. The more sun these plants get, the stronger their aromas will be.

HERB CHOICES FOR PARTIAL SUN & PARTIAL SHADE

Angelica, chervil, parsley, peppermint, sorrel, comfrey, wild strawberry, echinacea, eyebright and Lady's mantle.

These herbs grow best in dappled sunlight, out of the glare of full sun. In the wild their natural habitat is often at the edges of woods, where the canopy of trees is less dense, but still offers protection.

HERB CHOICES FOR FULL SHADE

St. John's wort, evening primrose, lungwort, valerian and sweet violet.

These herbs do not need full sunlight, and tend to have rich green leaves.

MINDFUL GARDENING

Plants communicate through scent. The smell of freshly cut grass is a call for help. Flowers make scents that call to their specific pollinators, some sweet as vanilla (literally) and some distasteful (to us) as rotten flesh. Farmers historically used scent (and also taste) to determine the make-up and health of soil. We can still tell if soil contains lots of clay or organic material from its scent. The former smells dusty and damp, whilst the latter is sweeter and might smell mossy or like leaf litter, sort of like the frog terrarium at the botanic gardens. Soil that has too much ammonia or that smells rotten or swampy might indicate the need for aeration and added compost. We can add that to the list of mindful gardening tasks: besides plant smellers, we need soil smellers. Perhaps it's not a full-time job, but taking time to smell your soil, your plants and the compost in your garden will likely tell you something you don't have to search for online to understand. The scents speak to a primal relationship with the land.

CITY BIRDS

Our cities are unnatural environments: noisy, crowded canyons of concrete, glass and metal. Whether we visit them to work, shop or travel it is easy to become overwhelmed by the frantic pace, volume and relentless energy of city life.

But take time to pause and step away from the crowds. Find a quiet space for a few moments and you'll begin to notice that nature is thriving here. Many birds live amongst the bustle and commotion of our cities. And these birds have all had to adapt to survive in this seemingly unfriendly habitat. Notice their behaviour and consider what they are seeking in a city.

For many birds, our cities provide a reliable source of food. Our leftover scraps provide sustenance for some species. Feral pigeons brazenly dance around our feet seemingly invisible to people rushing through the crowded streets. House sparrows are not as confident and will wait cautiously until we vacate our benches to swoop in and clear up our crumbs. The human desire to interact with nature is heightened in this urban environment and many people feed birds in city parks. The tamer birds reap the rewards, but other species still proudly retain their 'wildness' and do not approach humans, preferring to daringly race in, snatch food and retreat. Sit for a while and observe each species' strategy.

Don't forget to look up. To birds, our skyscrapers and office blocks are just cliff faces and their balconies and ledges provide potential nesting sites. You may glimpse a peregrine falcon, the ultimate aerial predator. Our cities supply the peregrine with its preferred nesting habitat (inaccessible ledges) and favourite food (pigeons), as such and this incredible falcon has successfully colonized cities the world over.

In colder months, a city centre is warmer than the surrounding countryside. Some birds will fly in to cities at night, meeting others of the same species, and form flocks that roost communally on city trees and ledges. These birds huddle close together sharing body warmth and communicating with dense chattering.

The bright city lights create a far-reaching glow that can act as a nocturnal navigation beacon to migrating birds overhead. Listen. Above the city's hum, can you hear the thin whistles high in the night sky? These are contact calls of reassurance between birds migrating somewhere up there amongst the stars.

For birds, a city can offer unique opportunities, food and community. Their reasons for choosing city life are not so different to our own.

WILD CHAMOMILE
Matricaria chamomilla

Chamomile was cultivated as early as the Neolithic period and has been used for centuries as a 'cure-all' medicinal plant. It is a great companion plant, as its strong, aromatic flowers attract beneficial insects that feed on pest predators, such as aphids. May is the perfect month to launch or plant chamomile seeds.

STEMS Branched, upright, smooth stem

LEAVES The long and narrow alternate leaves can be harvested fresh from the plant for medicinal uses.

FLOWERS Yellow and comb-like centres, surrounded by 10–20 white petals. Harvest the flowers for medicinal uses when open and fresh or dry for later use. It takes 20–35 days from flower to seed.

SEEDS 1 mm/$\frac{1}{25}$ inch elongated, light brown and ridged

LAUNCH SEEDBOMBS April–May and August–September

GERMINATION TIME 1–2 weeks

HARVESTING SEEDS Seeds ripen July–September

PLANT CARE Don't cut back the foliage before flowering as the flower production will reduce dramatically. To remove aphids wash off with a strong jet of water.

PESTS AND DISEASES Can suffer aphid attacks, which attract hungry ladybirds. Generally disease-free but susceptible to rust, downy mildew and powdery mildew.

CULINARY AND MEDICINAL USES Chamomile has soothing properties and is used to help alleviate conditions such as nervousness, anxiety, hysteria, headaches, stomach pains, indigestion, colds and flu. Also used as a poultice for swellings, sprains and bruises. Steep for fifteen minutes then drink for a gentle sleep aid.

FAMILY Asteraceae/Compositae

NATIVE TO Southern Europe

HEIGHT/SPREAD 60 x 40 cm/23⅝ x 15¾ inches

HABITAT Roadsides, railways, waste ground, fields, arable land

THRIVES IN Full sun/partial shade

SOIL Most soil types; tolerates poor soils

LIFESPAN Annual

FLOWERS May–August

FORM Upright

LEAF FORM Upper: Bipinnate; Lower: Tripinnate

POLLINATED BY Insects

WINGED WONDERS MEDITATION

You are standing in a field of wildflowers, beautiful gems of all the colours of the rainbow. It's the height of summer but there's a hint of a breeze, enough to make the tiny blooms bend and weave. They look like dancing fireflies. The air is sweet, and you draw in a deep invigorating breath, taking it into your lungs. You are buzzing with energy, so much so that you begin to run, skipping through the undergrowth in no particular direction. You imagine you're a feather caught in the wind. Around and around you spin, arms outstretched.

A bee hums its melody in your ear and you're suddenly aware of all the winged insects flitting and hovering, jumping from flower to flower. Butterflies with delicate gossamer wings and huge eye-shaped patterns dance before you. Dragonflies with their metallic wings join in the parade, swapping partners and directions with the flick of a tail. A turquoise damselfly circles you, a darting ribbon of light leading you in a pirouette. All the creatures of the Earth, of Mother Nature, have come to perform for you. Suddenly you want to join in with their capers and be a part of the show, to create something out of nothing, like these winged wonders on display. But what talents do you have and where to start?

As if in answer to your question, a translucent butterfly lands in the palm of your hand. Its wings are deeply veined and the colour of pearl. As you look again, you notice that it's changing form, transforming before your eyes. The wings are gone, the body is solid and lengthy, and you realize you are now holding a paintbrush. Your palm tingles with excitement. This is your chance to create something new. To paint your own portrait and make it real. Your fingers twitch and soon you are working away, using the air in front of you as your easel and canvas. You see with your imagination. There's no thought behind it, you let your innate creativity take over. Your wrist flicks as you splash swirls of light with an invisible palette. A pattern emerges, a carnival of colour and movement as the painting takes shape in your mind. Only you know what it is, the subject is of your choosing. Around you, the winged wonders gather to watch. They know something special is about to happen.

When you are ready, you take a step back. Pause to survey your masterpiece. It is a work of art because it comes from your soul. It captures the very essence of who you are. Inside you feel a flicker of warmth. The creative spark has been ignited.

The picture becomes a reality, not just a figment of your imagination, but flesh and blood. Framed and catching the sunlight it stands upon the grass and you marvel at your creation. The more you gaze at it, the bigger it becomes. Growing until it is no longer a portrait, but a portal the size of a window. Instinctively you step through, into your picture. You find yourself in a world of your own making. Everything feels comfortable here. There is nothing to fear because you know this place inside out. This is the seat of your imagination, the place where all things start.

You smile and say *'I am a creative being!'*

WINGED WONDERS
AFFIRMATION

Time may be ebbing, bringing this day to a close, but there is always another one waiting on the brow of the hill. A chance to start the story again, to let your creativity flow and express who you are. As night falls and you settle under the veil of stars, you feel at peace. You are ready to unleash your imagination and make your mark on the world.

I ignite my creative spark.

*There is potential in
every moment.*

I see with my imagination.

*Every day is an opportunity
to express myself.*

THE ECOLOGICAL HIGHWAY

When one island garden takes root near another, things get exciting. Your garden is part of a network of other gardens, containing diverse flowering plant species that can support an even wider range of pollinators. So not only do they allure wildlife to your outdoor space, they also connect you with other gardens in the city. How cool it is to be able to imagine your island of wild as part of one ecological highway, working in unison with all the other nearby window boxes, pots, gardens and parks. If your garden is close to an allotment or food-growing project, or even a couple of apple trees, it is helping pollinate fruit and vegetables growing in these spaces because bees, for instance, will transport pollen grains as they move from one flower to another. It's a neighbourly act, the perfect altruistic gesture. But it is also a meditation on how interconnected we are. Our pollinators need us but they are also one of our most precious resources, indispensable to almost all the flowering plants on Earth for reproduction. Without them, countless fruits, vegetables and nuts, as well as oils, fibres and raw materials, simply wouldn't exist. So whilst our city gardens may be small, they keep us in touch with these momentous ideas.

PUTTING PLANTS TOGETHER

Companion planting is about marrying plants that work well together in order to survive and grow strong and healthy. It is a gardener's and farmer's way of creating a botanical community where all plants benefit one another and the garden as a living organism.

CHOOSING PLANTS

Here are some of the different companion planting techniques for different plant requirements.

NATURE'S PESTICIDES These are plants that are known to deter pests like aphids; attract pollinators; and release toxins through their roots. The toxins remain in the soil for over a year and kill pest nematodes that can destroy the root system on host plants. Example: marigold (*Calendula officinalis*) is one of the most popular companion plants to grow for these reasons.

TRAP CROPPING One plant acts as a 'trap' to draw pests away from the main crop. Example: grow nasturtiums with roses and lettuces to attract aphids away.

ROOM TO GROW Plant beneficial weeds alongside plants that have weak root systems. The weeds naturally 'till' the soil, allowing the main crop to send its roots down deeper into the soil. Example: grow clover with tomatoes or corn.

ATTRACT BENEFICIALS Grow insectary plants that produce nectar and pollen to attract pollinators like bees, butterflies and hoverflies and the beneficial ladybirds to control aphid pests. Example: fennel, sunflower, lemon balm.

FLAVOUR BOOSTER Some herbs can make subtle changes to the flavour of neighbouring plants. Example: interplant basil with your tomatoes and the flavour of both will improve.

PROTECTION AND SUPPORT Some taller, denser plants can provide growing support, shade and shelter for vulnerable plants. By choosing plants that are low growing and have large leaves for a living mulch, you are helping to suppress weeds, keeping the soil cool and preventing moisture evaporation whilst also providing shade for vulnerable roots of plants. For example: you can grow large-leaved squash with onions.

STRONG SMELLS Some plants repel insect pests with their scent. Aroma can also be used to mask the scent of your main crop, hiding them from predators. Example: intercrop onions and leeks with your carrots to confuse carrot flies.

SOIL CONDITIONING Some plants can capture and release nutrients into the soil, making them available to their neighbours. Plants from the Leguminosae family, like clover, beans and peas, fix nitrogen in the soil, supplying the roots of other plants. Example: mustard (*sinapis alba*) suppresses soil-borne diseases and conditions the soil. Intercrop clover with your nitrogen-hungry crops, like cabbage.

LYRA

GREEK FOR: *lyre*

Represents the lyre, a musical instrument with strings. Lyra, a small but bright constellation, belongs to the Hercules (or Heracles in Greek) family of constellations. It's the host of the bright star Vega (α Lyrae). Vega was actually the North Star between 12,000 and 10,000 BCE and will become the North Star again around 14,000 CE due to the precession of the Earth's rotational axis. It was also the first star other than the sun to be photographed (by William Bond and John Adams Whipple in 1850) and the first one to have its spectrum recorded (by Henry Draper in 1872).

The name Vega is derived from an Arabic term that was translated into Latin as, Vultur Cadens, (the 'Falling Eagle' or 'Falling Vulture'). The constellation was represented as a vulture in ancient Egypt, and as an eagle or vulture in ancient India.

Beta Lyrae is a binary star system in the Lyra constellation. Its two stars orbit so close together that they have become egg-shaped and material flows from one to the other. The secondary star, originally the less massive of the two, has accreted so much mass that it is now substantially more massive. Another famous star towards the east of the constellation is called RR Lyrae, and is the prototype of a class of stars known as RR Lyrae variables. These are pulsating stars that act as 'standard candles' and make reliable markers to calculate distances in space.

CELESTIAL EVENTS

· Lyrids – *21–22 April* (originating from
  Comet Thatcher)
· Eta Lyrids – *9 May*
· June Lyrids – *15–16 June*

DEEP-SKY OBJECTS

· M56 (NGC 6779) – globular cluster
· Ring Nebula (M57, NGC 6720) – planetary
  nebula (second ever discovered and one of
  the best known)

SUMMER

JUNE

JULY

AUGUST

JUNE

Time to be you. Wild camping and picnics mean mindful times with the people that help us bloom.

FORAGING

URBAN FORAGING

As we grow older, as we get busier and more stressed out, we acquire deftness to our physicality, but we miss out on so many experiences of touch, experiences that can inform us about the shape of our environment. It is crucial for our wellbeing, however, to try to retain that sense of wonder through sensory activities – and especially so in our urban surroundings, when we are often simply trying to get through a to-do list as efficiently as we can. When we tune into our senses, we see that feeling joy in a place isn't always just an intellectual pursuit, but one in which the hands can make contact with the city itself; its shape, texture, how warm or cool it is, how soft or hard. The appeal of foraging is down to the repetitive, rhythmic action of picking from plants. It holds a hypnotic quality that allows the physical act to fill the moment. It is a time when your hands seem to lead your head, for a change – so that the only thought swimming through your mind is a respect for, and curiosity about, the complex chemistry that created the squidgy, auburn berry pinched between your fingers.

Not all cities are so well-stocked in edible plants. But we can turn our hands to plenty of other pursuits that offer that same tangible connection to the urban environment, where the pleasure of a thing is registered by the fingers before the brain. Botanic gardens and public parks are the obvious candidates. But fountains, sculptures and old brickwork can also offer us sensory pleasure. Running one's hand through a lively jet of water as it sparkles in the sunlight is a playful, childlike pleasure – and, moreover, this action of reaching out is instinctive to us to perform, bringing a simple enjoyment that can also ground us.

BEETS
Beta vulgaris

Beets are a versatile crop and relatively easy to grow. You can grow them well in the ground or in a container and harvest them small or large. If you choose the right cultivar, they can withstand some frost, too.

PLANTING TIPS

Each visible beet seed actually contains two or three inner seeds, so sow thinner to take account of this.

CULTIVATION

Choose a sunny site and provide plenty of water early on when the root starts to swell, about eight weeks after sowing. In hot conditions, they tend to go to seed (bolt); regular but not excessive watering helps to prevent this.

WEED CONTROL

Beet crops are reasonably tolerant of weeds, but it is important to do at least one hand weed at the seedling stage. After that, using a hoe is the quickest way, but be careful to avoid damaging the roots.

TIP
*Space in
containers is precious,
so what you can do is sow
thickly and then harvest the
majority as baby salad greens or
baby beets. Leave a few of the
strongest seedlings to grow
into mature beets.*

LIFESPAN Two or three seasons; if left, it will flower and set seed in year two

PLANT Can be sown any time from spring to early autumn

GROW IN Fertile, well-drained soil in the open ground or in containers

ECO-REFLECTION

IN CONTEMPLATION
OF WATER

Observing water in motion makes you mindful of what is required in the present moment. When it is time to do so, water rolls and runs; when stillness is called for, it rests. It also reminds us that letting go of emotional and physical baggage helps to keep the spirit light, because water does not cling – its surface reflects the moment for as long as it endures. A river will tolerate all that travels with it, both beautiful and ugly – shoals of fish, tin cans, pebbles and weeds – but is attached to none. Water is part of us, an essential and major component of our physiology. This is why its presence and sound has a calming and uplifting effect on us, in whatever form it appears. After all, the element is life-giving and life-sustaining – qualities possessed by rain in equal measure. So as it is soaking you to the bone, try to remember how vital it is. Try to accept its inconvenience as a reminder of our lack of control over many things, and remember it is sometimes better to accept than to fight an unwelcome downpour. In simply knowing that there is little you can do to avoid getting wet, you may even find you enjoy the sensation of water tickling your skin.

Psychologists encourage us to tolerate uncertainty in life with unconditional acceptance. Our wellbeing, they believe, depends upon it and is further served by being able to see ourselves as a part of an interconnected whole. We can't change the weather but, wearing the right clothing or not, it is healthy to embrace that which comes our way.

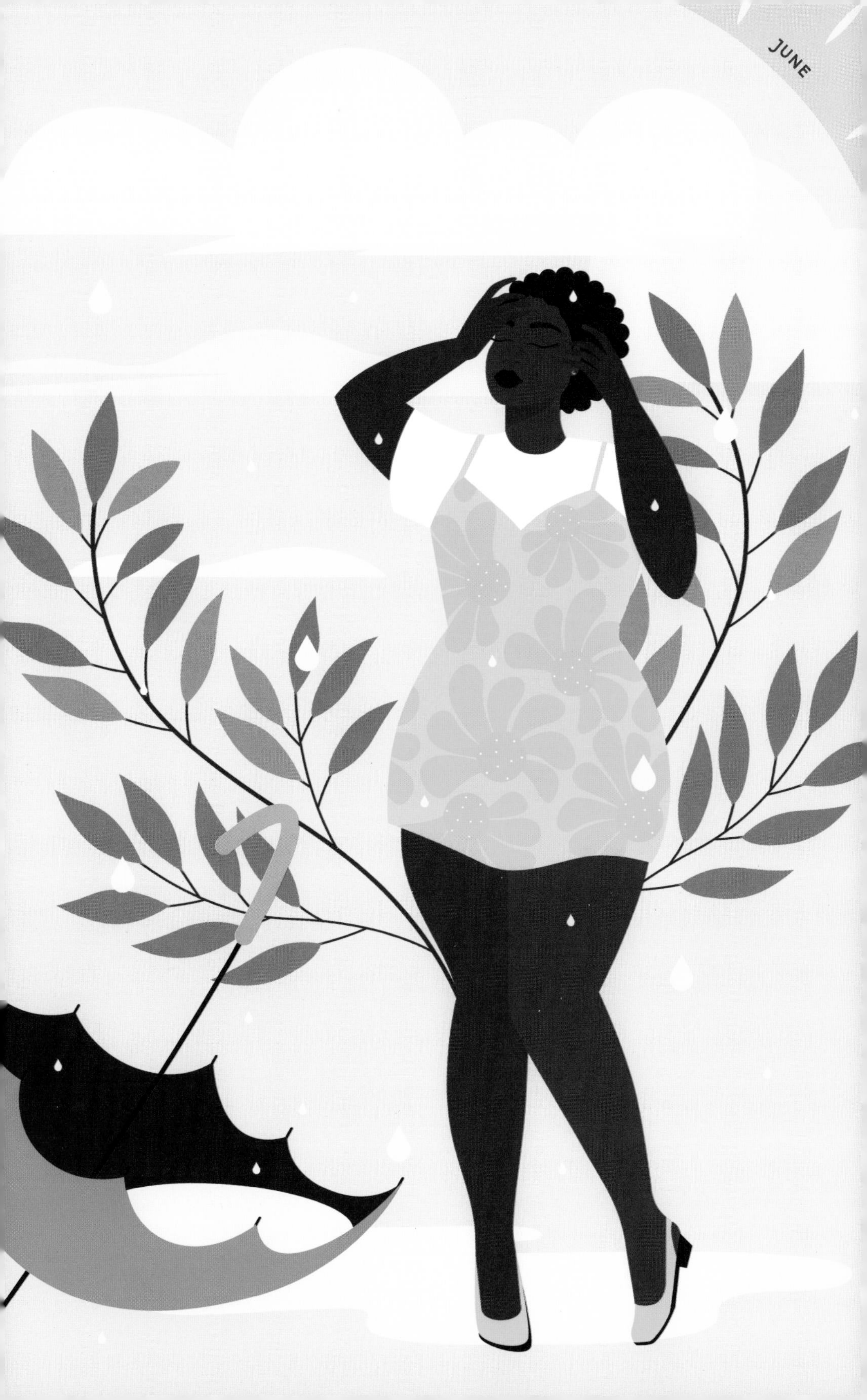
JUNE

TOMATOES
Solanum lycopersicum

There's really no reason not to grow tomatoes. With the right choice of variety, they will taste vastly superior to those you buy in shops. They are relatively easy to grow, although feeding and watering is important.

PLANTING TIPS

You can sow the seeds in flats or flowerpots and then transplant the stronger seedlings into individual flowerpots to continue growing. You can also transplant them into a larger flowerpot before planting into their final space in the ground. They will root from the stem, so plant them a little deeper to allow for a larger root area.

CULTIVATION

Tomatoes need rich soil, but if your soil is not there yet, you can supplement with a natural liquid fertilizer high in potassium and phosphorus. Water with a solution of this once the flowers start to form. Avoid high-nitrogen fertilizers because they will make the growth sappy, lush and susceptible to disease and pest attack.

Regular but not excessive watering is essential if you want to avoid split fruit. Stop watering in autumn to help prevent fungal diseases as the weather gets cooler and damper. Remove the lower leaves as they start to discolour; this allows for the plant to put all its energy into the younger, productive growth and the developing fruit. Support the growth as the plants begin to grow upwards by tying to stakes or bamboo canes, and remove the side shoots of vine tomatoes so that only the main stem grows up the support.

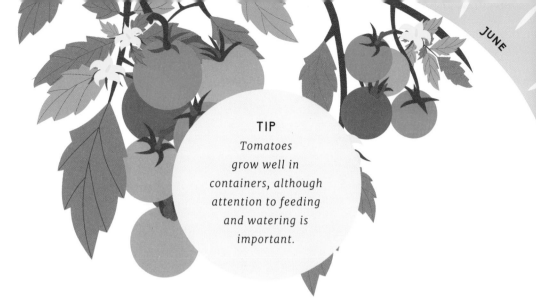

TIP
*Tomatoes
grow well in
containers, although
attention to feeding
and watering is
important.*

WEED CONTROL

Keep weeds at bay, especially at the early stages. Young plants can
be planted through a black plastic sheet, or you can cover them with
a layer of organic mulch. Try undersowing with marigolds
(Calendula officinalis); as well as smothering weeds, marigolds are also
said to attract beneficial insects that can deter some pests.

HARVEST

Harvest regularly. If you are eating the fruit immediately, then leave
it on until completely ripe. Pick a couple of days early if you need to
transport or keep the fruit. At the end of the season, pick any green
tomatoes and bring them indoors for ripening in a warm place.

LIFESPAN Three seasons

PLANT Sow indoors at 15–30°C/59–86°F six to eight weeks
before last expected frost date

GROW IN Most well-drained, fertile soil is suitable; in cool
climates, they do better in a protected tunnel or greenhouse

CARING FOR YOUR CROPS

Mature plants will need a bit of TLC – pruning, clipping and weeding where necessary, regular watering and feeding. And some taller plants may need staking if winds are high, or climbers may need tying in as they grow up their poles and trellises. Trimmed and damaged parts of a plant can be composted and diseased parts can be burned and used as a potash around your fruit trees to give them an extra potassium boost.

FEEDING

The theory behind companion planting (see page 118) suggests that the necessary feeding of your plants may be reduced as you will be partnering your crops with companions that feed the soil. But it is best to back this up by using your homemade green manures and animal manures and in these you will find the three main nutrients most plants need to stay vigorous. Nitrogen (N), phosphorus (P) and potassium (K).

PROTECTION

A companion garden still needs a little help with 'big' pest prevention, such as rabbits, cats and birds, and protection from the elements, and it can be fun making things for this out of recycled unwanted items. Seedlings and plantlets need protection from being eaten or trampled on to help them establish into strong worldly plants. This can be done by simply building a frame to fit the space and securing netting or a horticultural fleece cloche. So long as whatever you use allows water and light in but keeps pests out, you're on to a winner. Frames can be made with wood or bendy polypipe. Do make sure you bury the edges of the fleece or net to prevent hungry pests from climbing under.

SCARING BIRDS

We've come a long way from the humble scarecrow and now he has many bird-scaring accomplices in the garden. These days there is a multitude of innovative eco bird scaring designs and most of them involve the use of bamboo canes, something colourful and sparkly, and string! Simply drive some bamboo canes into the ground around your crops and tie colourful fabric or CDs and shells, or even cutlery and old gardening hand tools, and when the wind carries them in a gust the birds will soon flee.

TIN CAN CLOCHE

Another great idea for pest prevention is to sow seeds or plant your seedlings then cover with a recycled tin can with the bottom cut out. It helps to create a warm environment and prevents slugs and snails, foraging birds and small mammals from devouring your plants. Remove the tin can once the plants are big enough to fend for themselves.

Recycling what you have to hand is one of the best ways of creating barriers against pests and you can rest well knowing you are doing something good for the environment whilst protecting your crops.

BLUE MINDFULNESS

Contrary to the aim of mindfulness as inner contemplation, blue
mindfulness is an emptying out of oneself to achieve identification
with the ocean. It is a mindfulness that mirrors the ocean's expressions
of ever-changing surface turbulence and deep unseen currents.
These expressions can be compared to the twin capacities of vigilant
and paradoxical attention. You wait patiently for a wave, like a seabird
ready to penetrate the oily skin of the sea. You can identify with the
seabird through your vigilant attention – a constant round of watching
and then acting – as the bird plunges underwater and reappears
a moment later with a wriggling fish in its silver beak. At the same time
you are exerting a deep scan, taking in the background colours and
textures of the sea; the fragrance of salt laden air within which you
are cocooned, all through paradoxical attention. The wave approaches
and unfurls. . .You are blue mindfulness, immersed in the joy of wave
watching with both a focused and a scanning, appreciative attention.

FIRST-AID PLANT POWER

Nature's kingdom is abundant in all sorts of powerful remedies for injuries, emergencies and life's ups and downs. Natural home remedies can be made for soothing and healing cuts, bruises, breaks and strains, and for treating everyday ailments like colds and flu, headaches, hayfever and tummy upsets.

HONEY & MARIGOLD GRAZE REMEDY

Try this remedy instead of painfully picking gravel out of a graze. Honey is antiseptic, with strong healing properties; combined with the amazing marigold, it makes for miraculous healing.

MAKES 340 G/12 OZ

INGREDIENTS

- 20 or so fresh marigold flowers (or 10 g/¹/₃ oz dried)
- 340 g/12 oz jar of runny honey

METHOD

Put the marigold flowers into a larger, sterilized jar. Pour the honey over them, up to the top. Leave it for 2–3 weeks, or until you need it (there is no need to take the flowers out of the honey). To use, slather the honey all over the grazed area. Cover with a large sticking plaster and leave overnight. The next day, carefully peel off the plaster. The honey will have pulled out all the tiny stones, leaving the wound clean. Keeps 1–2 years or more.

QUICK CHAMOMILE EYE POULTICE FOR SORE EYES

MAKES ENOUGH FOR ONE OR BOTH EYES

INGREDIENTS

- 1–2 chamomile tea bags
- 2 tbsp boiling water

METHOD

Place the tea bags in a small bowl and cover with the boiling water. When cooled to just warm, lightly drain the bags. Lie down and place the bags over closed eyes for 5–15 mins. For immediate use.

FINDING YOUR PLACE

Nature can be profoundly life-affirming, enhancing our creativity and freedom. It also has its dangerous, destructive side: every parent knows we need to provide careful guidance to ensure our child stays as safe as possible in nature, and doesn't stray too close to a rocky ledge, swim too far out to sea, or put their hand too close to a campfire.

Parents need to balance the roles of risk-taker and caretaker, walking the fine line between expanding borders and encouraging adventure, whilst setting safe boundaries so our children learn to respect nature. There are so many life skills that we can help our children to learn if we take the right approach to the great outdoors. Even if we live in cities and urban areas, we can introduce them to the awesome power of the natural elements with whatever form of nature is present around us. No matter where we are, there is always at least one or two of these elements present and they have different qualities to explore and enjoy wholeheartedly.

Think about what natural scenes you have the best access to. Maybe you have city parks, or perhaps there are rivers, woods, forests, hills or mountains with caves to explore together nearby or if you go on holiday. Finding enjoyable ways of being in nature is a way of being mindful together, and will create memories that become a lifelong gift. When our awareness is absorbed by our contact with the world, we feel fully alive in body and mind and in direct contact with life itself.

JUNE

OBSERVING THE RHYTHM OF THE SKIES

Day by day, the rising time of each star shifts ever so slightly, as does the time of the sunrise and sunset. That shift is very precise – so much so that we have to add a leap second to our clocks every few years. The sun and moon follow their own rhythms, and rarer events such as meteor showers and eclipses add a certain syncopation to the heavenly beat.

Observation of the sky was first undertaken as a way of recording its rhythms and cycles, in order to create a calendar. In ancient times, astronomers were priests, and astronomical calculations were often preciously guarded secrets. In ancient China, the main responsibility of political power was to keep the Earth in harmony with the sky. This so-called 'Mandate of Heaven' meant that astronomers had influence over daily life as well as major political strategies. In ancient Greece, a solar eclipse around the year 600 BCE was predicted by the philosopher Thales and was interpreted as an omen. It interrupted a battle between the Medes and the Lydians and brought it to a truce. In many cultures, being able to predict astronomical events meant power. The Atharva Veda, a collection of hymns written in India around 1500 BCE, was one of the earliest texts that described rituals based on astronomical knowledge. Texts like this gave the rulers power to know exactly the right day to perform the right ritual to the right god to ensure they achieved their goal, whether that was winning a battle, fathering a son or making sure enough rain fell to water the crops.

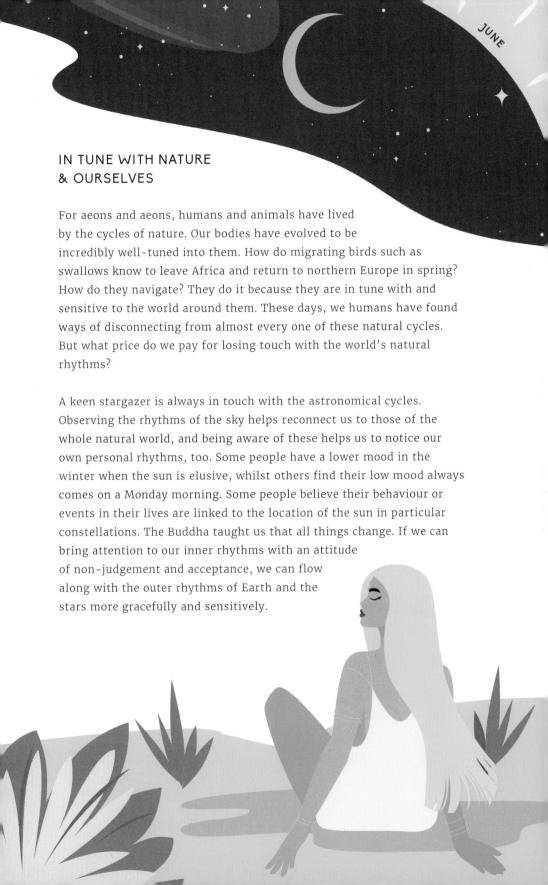

IN TUNE WITH NATURE
& OURSELVES

For aeons and aeons, humans and animals have lived
by the cycles of nature. Our bodies have evolved to be
incredibly well-tuned into them. How do migrating birds such as
swallows know to leave Africa and return to northern Europe in spring?
How do they navigate? They do it because they are in tune with and
sensitive to the world around them. These days, we humans have found
ways of disconnecting from almost every one of these natural cycles.
But what price do we pay for losing touch with the world's natural
rhythms?

A keen stargazer is always in touch with the astronomical cycles.
Observing the rhythms of the sky helps reconnect us to those of the
whole natural world, and being aware of these helps us to notice our
own personal rhythms, too. Some people have a lower mood in the
winter when the sun is elusive, whilst others find their low mood always
comes on a Monday morning. Some people believe their behaviour or
events in their lives are linked to the location of the sun in particular
constellations. The Buddha taught us that all things change. If we can
bring attention to our inner rhythms with an attitude
of non-judgement and acceptance, we can flow
along with the outer rhythms of Earth and the
stars more gracefully and sensitively.

THE POWER OF NATURE

Reconnecting with the natural world is reassuring and calms the soul.
The knowledge that deep down the Earth is still turning, the seasons
are changing and all is well with the world – this provides security
and helps to put into perspective our own often minor aggravations and
inconveniences that grow to dominate our lives.

Let the wild world call you to it – connect with your world and open
up a lifetime of opportunity and adventure. Moments such as these are
precious and privileged. They give us a profound feeling of connectedness
with our world and provide great perspective to our everyday lives. The
power and immensity of the nature that we encounter reminds us of our
insignificance in the grander scheme of things, and our humility and
wonder at the world reminds us of the responsibility we have to our wild
places and the value they have for our future health and prosperity.

JULY

*Time to be aware. Notice how nature
can make you feel. Nature bathing
is restorative and invigorating.*

WATERFALL MEDITATION

Behind you is a giant waterfall, it cascades down into a deep ravine where each droplet of water meets and becomes something new, just as your thoughts form ideas in your mind. With every step you take you feel more energized. You know that you can be anything you want, because you are the artist, the inventor, the force behind everything. Your reality is a result of all the choices you have made up until this moment, which means that every choice and action that follows creates a new destiny.

Nothing is impossible.

When you are ready you take a step back through the portal, through the picture and into your reality, but you are not alone. You bring inspiration and a renewed verve for life with you. Your imagination is on fire. The meadow greets you like an old friend, and you feel lucky to be alive. The sun is slipping from its place in the sky and everything is bathed in an amber glow. The subtle changes bring a different kind of beauty to the landscape and you realize that each moment has something new to offer. There is potential in every second.

Time may be ebbing, bringing this day to a close, but there is always another one waiting on the brow of the hill. A chance to start the story again, to let your creativity flow and express who you are. As night falls and you settle under the veil of stars, you feel at peace. You are ready to unleash your imagination and make your mark on the world.

TAKING YOUR CREATIVE WORK OUTSIDE

Taking our making work outside can be one of the most peaceful ways to experience a slower pace of life, combining the connectedness with Earth and the meaningfulness of using our hands. A hand-sewing kit, an outdoor hand-built kiln, a space for wood shavings to scatter, painting or sketching 'en plein air', taking castings for jewellery work – it doesn't matter what you do; if you are able to step outside to continue your work, you will find it highly beneficial. Using portable hand tools allows you the joy and freedom of working outdoors and is also a great way to create a quieter space for your making without the background whirr of machinery. Inspiration from nature can show up in our work in many ways, but using natural materials directly from our surrounding environment, such as leaves, clay, flowers or wood, connects us whilst sharing our story of where or how we fit in our own landscapes.

Of course, it is not always practical to take our materials and tools outside, but by aiming to create a space to work and indeed to live in a way that connects deeper with nature means that every day we have more of a chance of experiencing the benefits of 'forest bathing'. It could be filling a corner of your work space and home with potted plants, or opening the windows wider, or planting out a window box. In our modern world of built environments, small changes can help create pockets of mindfulness within our lives.

ECO-REFLECTION

NATURE – THE GREATEST MUSE

Actively spending time outside in nature helps us to slow down and
notice the minute details of life, the slow changing of the seasons, the
beauty in simple everyday things – an unfurling flower, clouds scudding
across a cerulean sky, a bird singing, the dusting of snow on a branch.
Teaching ourselves to look and truly see different aspects of nature helps
us to be part of our environment more fully, and guides us to slow our
days down so that we can enjoy these moments for longer and more
often. Learning to settle happily, contentedly, into the quiet of your
garden, a local park, a nearby forest or even just your balcony in order to
soak up the inspiration means that you are doing less seeking in the noisy
world, and more being in the real world.

ENCHANTED GARDEN

It's a beautiful summer's evening. The scent of honeysuckle fills the air. You are walking by the side of a walled garden. Climbing tea roses scale the stone; they sprawl in every direction, peppering the wall with hints of pink, yellow and luminous white. The birds accompany you on your journey. They twitter their delicate song above your head. The path you've chosen meanders in no particular direction, but that's OK. You feel relaxed and trust that nature will lead you where you need to be.

Up ahead you see a door nestled in the wall. It is carved from oak and engraved with vines and butterflies. You wonder what lies behind this door, what is waiting for you on the other side. You reach out, touch the grain of the wood. It feels smooth, ancient, filled with secrets. Gently you push. The huge brass hinges of the door creak, as it glides open and you are bathed in golden sunshine.

You step forwards into the light, unable at first to see anything, but gradually your sight adjusts and you take in your surroundings. You are standing in the centre of a magical garden. Fluted blooms cluster between majestic sunflowers, their vibrant faces turned upwards. Bushes littered with pretty pink and purple flowers seem to vibrate with the heavy hum of bees at work. Trees enclose the entire space, some small, just finding their first leaves, whilst others tower over the scene, their wide, glossy leaves cloaking the garden in a wash of deep green. Ferns trail around worn stone planters filled with pansies and petunias, whilst willowy irises sway in the borders. Wherever you look you see something new and delightful. The joys of summer fill your heart and you long to stay in this place forever.

But just as this thought arises, so the scenery shifts, and you find
you are part of a different picture. The light flickers from summer
brightness to a deeper, richer tone. There's warmth in these amber
hues but also a nip to the air, a chill that seeps under your skin.
The ground beneath your feet seems to ripple and then harden, and
for a moment you feel out of place, unsure and unsteady. You take a
breath, draw down the energy of the Earth and feel it anchoring you
in place. Just as the shrubs and trees are tethered by nature, so are you;
connected to all things and in harmony with the seasons.

The leaves crisp before your eyes, the luscious emerald tones turn yellow
and then lighten, becoming orange and red. Glowing fronds of autumn
brightness greet you at every turn. The flowers are now almost gone, but
the colour is still spectacular. Tendrils of wind ruffle your hair, picking
up leaves and twigs in a swirl which dances before your eyes, but you do
not move. You are rooted to the spot. In perfect
balance with the world around you.

Then just as quickly as it first began, this symphony is over. The blaze of colour fades, and the shadows of winter sneak in. You can feel them working their way into the space before your eyes. Dark, spectral, but exquisite in the way they change the atmosphere. The leaves have disappeared. The skeletal trees strike a pose against an almost white backdrop. Plants withdraw into themselves and the soil to be replenished. All is calm, just like your breathing. A thin layer of frost adds the finishing touch, making everything glisten and the chill sets in.
It gnaws at your bones and reminds you that you are alive, that you can feel and think and be energized by the icy cold, just as the warmth of the sun lifts your spirits. There is a time and a place for everything. Light and dark, black and white. Nature is in balance.

Spring is around the corner; in a heartbeat it beckons. Beneath your feet you feel it coming. New life stirs in the womb of the Earth. It trembles, and you feel a rush of excitement and anticipation at what is to come. The first shoots appear, pushing through the soil. Blades of grass spring up at every turn and you marvel at the changes. At the ebb and flow of life. Bushes unfurl, their stems filled with buds. Trees brighten, reaching for the sun as their canopy of leaves sprout and thicken. The cycle moves on, from old to new, from yin to yang.

It is time now for you to go, but you do not leave the enchanted garden with nothing. You carry with you a thought, a truth that you will keep with you, always.

The Earth anchors me.

*I am in perfect balance
with nature.*

*I am exactly where
I need to be.*

*My mind, body and
soul are in harmony.*

A SENSE OF PLACE

When remembering a place or describing a landscape, the senses are particularly important. The sense of smell, which doesn't tend to be used very prominently in writing, in real life can carry us straight back to a place in our distant memory. Where does the scent of lavender take you; or mown grass; or freshly washed cotton? When trying to recall a particular memory – a childhood picnic, for example – we may think first of the people, games and activities of the day. But if we really want to take ourselves there in memory, we can quietly engage the imagination and slip back into the bodies we had then: feel the grass underfoot, taste those sandwiches, hear mother's voice.

Stop and take a couple of quiet breaths.

Close your eyes for a moment and then open them again. What do you see? What is ahead of you, and what is on the periphery of your vision?

Concentrate on your hearing. Even in a quiet area there may be something in the distance: the drone of traffic, a bird singing, the sound of your own heart beating.

What are you touching? Think about what you can feel even without actively touching – perhaps the air temperature, a breeze, the grass beneath your feet, some physical sensation.

Can you taste anything? Coffee perhaps? The lingering flavour of your last meal? Toothpaste?

Give attention to your sense of smell. This is often the neglected or unnoticed. Are there any obvious scents or odours around you? If not, cup your hands over your nose and mouth and describe what you can smell.

THYME
Thymus vulgaris

A low-growing perennial up to 45 cm/18 inches tall, thyme has woody stems and tiny, twig-like branches forming a dense mat of tiny, dark green, aromatic leaves. Spikes of pinkish flowers occur in high summer. The whole plant is very attractive to bees, butterflies and other beneficial insects. There are many varieties – for example, *thymus serpyllum* and *thymus pulegoides* have larger, more oval leaves, whilst *thymus citriodorus* is lemon-scented. It is best to grow thyme plants from a reputable supplier to get the right species – once established, cuttings can be taken from a parent plant. All thyme needs well-drained, preferably sandy soil, with as much sun and heat as possible. Native to the southern Mediterranean region, plants also grow well in rock gardens and tolerate drought. Although the leaves can be harvested all year round, the flavour is best in high summer when the volatile-oil content is highest.

The ancient Greeks burned thyme as a purifying incense to cleanse temples and homes. The name thyme may be linked to the Greek word 'thumos', meaning courage – the powerful aroma has long been appreciated for its positive effects on the mind. Roman writers praised thyme as a fumigator and antiseptic. The plant is likely to have been introduced into Britain by the Romans.

PART OF PLANT USED Leaves

ACTIVE INGREDIENTS Bitters, flavonoids, saponins, tannins, volatile oil

COMMERCIALLY AVAILABLE AS Fresh and dried herb, capsules, lozenges, liniment, cough medicine

ACTIONS Antimicrobial, antiseptic, expectorant, vulnerary

USED TO TREAT

- SORE THROATS, HOARSENESS OF VOICE: lozenges can be sucked, or an infusion of fresh leaves, cooled, can be used as a gargle to soothe and fight infection
- COUGHS: cough medicine taken as directed, or a warm infusion of fresh leaves with a teaspoon of honey, eases spasmodic coughs
- POOR CIRCULATION, MUSCULAR ACHES AND PAINS: liniment applied to aching muscles 2–3 times daily warms and improves circulation

CULINARY USE Add to meat or fish dishes, and to root vegetables such as carrots; macerate in herbal vinegars and oils.

SAFETY INFORMATION Thyme is not advised medicinally in pregnancy because it can stimulate menstruation. Culinary use is safe.

THE PRINCIPLES OF ZERO-WASTE GARDENING

Most of us don't have unlimited space for growing food. Choosing what to grow and making the best use of it once we have grown it can be quite tricky. Here are a few things to consider.

SPACE

Zero-waste gardening means good planning; for each feature crop, there will be a guide to how much space one plant takes up and the yield you can expect. This will help you grow as much as possible of the crops you like, in the space you have.

WASTE

It is important to grow what you need and make sure you pick and eat it. If you are away in the summer, don't grow crops that only fruit whilst you are on holiday. When you have too much to eat all in one go, freezing, drying, pickling and fermenting can help hang on to those gluts until you are ready to eat them.

TASTE

One of the great benefits of growing your own food is that it often tastes better. Which are the crops that really deliver flavour when you grow your own? Leafy vegetables are a must as they deteriorate so quickly once picked. Tomatoes, corn, and peas are just a few of the others that are worth finding space for in your zero-waste garden.

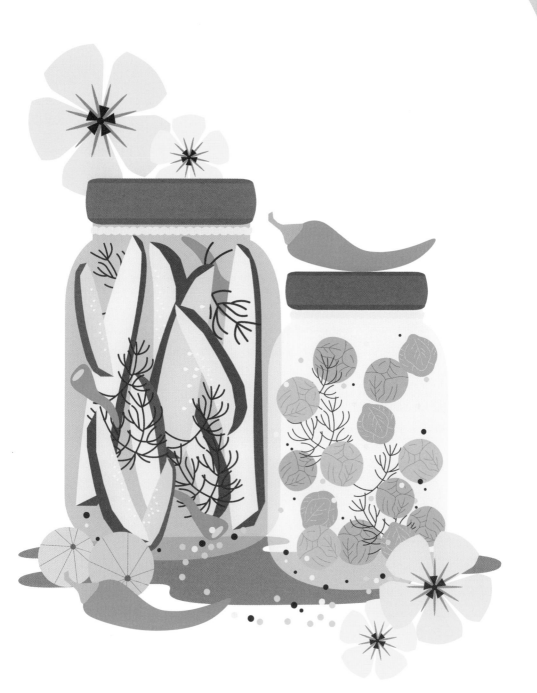

GROWING

STRAWBERRIES
Fragaria

Quick to fruit and easy to grow, strawberries are wonderful container plants. Being small and hardy, you can even grow them in small containers, provided they have enough food and water.

PLANTING TIPS
Plant in spring to give the plants time to get established by winter, but if you live in a mild-winter area, an early autumn planting will bring fruit the next summer.

CULTIVATION
Keep the plants well watered, but avoid overhead watering whilst the fruit develops because this may cause them to rot. Using a balanced liquid fertilizer at this time will improve the quality and quantity of the fruit. Remove runners as they appear, unless you are propagating them for more plants. Strawberries are prone to slug damage, and when they turn red, they are readily picked at by birds, so protect the crop with netting.

You can keep growing strawberry plants for a few years, but as they get older, the fruit tends to get smaller. This means more picking for the same quantity of fruit. For this reason, as well as avoiding disease build up, replanting is generally recommended every three years or so.

WEED CONTROL

Strawberries don't compete that well with weeds, so they are usually grown through a mulch of either straw or a woven plastic sheet. This not only helps to retain moisture, but it also protects the fruit. In late winter or early spring, tidy the plants by removing the old foliage and taking out any weeds by hand.

HARVEST

When the time comes, pick the fruit often, and always remove rotten or half-eaten fruit because these will cause disease problems for the remaining crop.

LIFESPAN Two or three years, then replace old plants with fresh stock

PLANT Grow from plants in spring; in mild-winter areas, plant in early autumn

GROW IN A rich, moist soil in full sun

RECIPE FOR CONNECTION

STRAWBERRY RHUBARB PIE

Pies are for sharing and are usually made from the freshest fruits. They connect us to both people and planet in one sweet bite. The ingredients in this pie help to recall our dependence on the natural world. If you grow the strawberries or rhubarb yourself, that then makes us feel a part of nature. Do avoid rhubarb leaves though, as they are poisonous.

SERVES 6–8

INGREDIENTS

PASTRY
- 320 g/11¾ oz all-purpose flour
- 175/6 oz butter
- 1 tbsp honey
- 1 tsp orange peel
- Pinch of salt
- 1 egg
- 2 tsp white wine vinegar
- 50 ml/2 fl oz ice cold water

FILLING
- 500 g/18 oz chopped rhubarb
- 500 g/18 oz washed and cut strawberries
- 300 g/10 oz beet sugar
- 1 tbsp all-purpose flour
- ½ tsp ground cinnamon
- 1 tsp vanilla extract or vanilla sugar
- 3 tbsp butter

TIP

*You need
at least 1 hour of
kitchen time to
make a pie*

METHOD

Preheat your oven to 220°C/200°C fan/425° F/gas 7.

1. Blend the flour, butter, honey, orange peel and salt together using two forks. Criss-cross the forks until your dough looks like tiny pebbles. In a separate bowl, whisk together the egg, vinegar and water. Then, pour this into your dry ingredients bowl and stir the mixture together until you form a large, soft ball of dough. Divide your dough ball in half. Roll out one piece with a rolling pin and place it in your lightly greased pie dish. Place your pie dish and your other dough ball in the fridge to chill for atleast 2 hours.

2. Mix together the rhubarb, strawberries, beet sugar, flour, cinnamon and vanilla in a large bowl and then pour it into your chilled crust. Dot the top of the filling with the butter.

3. Now roll out the other piece of dough. You can roll out onesolid piece and then cut into strips to place them on top of your filling in a criss-cross lattice shape. You can use the left over dough to decorate the top of your pie.

4. Once you've made and executed your pie top, make sure you've cut a few air strips on the top so the filling can breathe, and also crimped the edges so the filling doesn't leak out the sides. Before you put your pie in the oven, wrap tin foil around the edges of the pie as they have a tendency to burn.

5. Pop it in the oven for 15 minutes. Then, reduce the temperature to 190°C/170°C fan/375° F/gas 5 for another 45 minutes.

AUGUST

*Time to be enchanted. Sunrises,
sunflowers and sunsets are
mindful and magical.*

BE LIKE WATER

In the *Tao Te Ching*, the Chinese sage Lao Tzu celebrates the qualities of water: 'It benefits all things without contention. In dwelling, it stays grounded. In being, it flows to depths. In expression, it is honest. In confrontation, it stays gentle. In governance, it does not control. In action, it aligns to timing. It is content with its nature and therefore cannot be faulted.'

'The supreme goodness' – the highest state of moral life – 'is like water,' says Lao Tzu. It is shape-shifting and adaptable; it absorbs as it expresses. The most destructive of human traits is the inability to absorb contrasting views. Taoists do not look to metaphors of nature as instruction on how to live, but instead to direct instruction from nature. They believe we are a component of nature and nature is an expression of Tao.

The Taoists generally say that water is yin – absorbing, adaptable. But that is for the brook, the stream and the flat sea. Waves are more yang and 'tough'. They fight back. Then, water is relentless. It never stops. When restricted, it seeks the weakest spot of any obstruction and applies constant pressure until it is free. Water is opportunistic. Given the slightest opening, it will pass through. Water is a force as much as it is a presence.

*If you choose
the ocean as your teacher,
then do not turn your back
on it. Do what water asks;
in other words, flow.*

LEMON
Citrus limonum

Lemon trees are evergreen, and native species have large, sharp thorns protruding from branches. Commercial varieties have been bred to be free of thorns to help with harvesting. Major producing countries today include Brazil, Sicily and the United States. Lemon leaves are shiny and dark green on the upper surface and paler beneath, pitted with tiny sacs filled with volatile oil. The fragrant flowers are white. Yellow lemon fruit also has visible oil sacs in the peel; pare off a piece of lemon rind and turn it over to see them clearly. When these burst, the zesty lemon aroma is released.

Citrus trees originated in China, and due to early trade routes, cultivation spread into eastern and southern mediterranean regions in the fourteenth and fifteenth centuries, and then to the New World. In the sixteenth century, eating lemons was encouraged on English ships because they protected sailors from scurvy, a disease caused by lack of vitamin C.

PART OF PLANT USED Peel, leaves

ACTIVE INGREDIENTS Volatile oils

COMMERCIALLY AVAILABLE AS Fruit, essential oils

ACTIONS Antiseptic, astringent, diuretic, refreshing aroma

USED TO TREAT

- LOW IMMUNITY, INFLUENZA, COLDS: Add four drops of lemon essential oil to one pint of boiling water and inhale the steam for 10 minutes as a cleansing inhalation.

- OILY AND COMBINATION SKIN PROBLEMS: two drops of lemon essential oil added to one teaspoon of aloe vera gel massaged into the face at night clears the pores, heals spots and improves skin texture.

- DEPRESSION, LOW SELF-ESTEEM, ANXIETY: two drops of lemon essential oil on a Kleenex, inhaled, uplifts low moods.

CULINARY USE Fresh lemon juice is commonly used with fish dishes, also as a salad dressing or in baking; lemon peel is a versatile flavouring in sweet and savoury recipes.

SAFETY INFORMATION Lemon essential oil from the peel used on the skin can cause irregular patches of pigmentation in UV light (phototoxity). Avoid skin use if exposure to sun is intended. Lemon leaf is safe for skin use in the sun.

THE CALL OF THE WILD

Take a step into nature and reignite your connection to it, see the world with a new perspective and nourish your soul. There is a certain soft focus that we can achieve through mindful running that allows us to see the world in a slightly different way. By letting go of the narrow focus of our minds a runner takes in the world through a slightly wider perspective, one that does not just see the brightest lights and the loudest sounds that usually draw all our attention. With this wider perspective, borne of mindfulness, we become aware of the silence between sounds and the shadows between shapes – the negative spaces in the world.

Let the wild world call you to it – connect with your world and open up a lifetime of opportunity and adventure. These moments give us a profound feeling of connectedness with our world and provide great perspective to our everyday lives. The power and immensity of the nature that we encounter reminds us of our insignificance in the grander scheme of things, and our humility and wonder at the world reminds us of the responsibility we have to our wild places and the value they have for our future health and prosperity.

CYGNUS

LATIN FOR: *swan*

The stars in Cygnus, the swan, form important asterisms in the night sky. The five brightest stars make up the Northern Cross (the body of the swan), with Deneb – the very brightest star – forming the 'tail'.

Deneb, together with Altair in the Aquila (Eagle) constellation and Vega in the Lyra constellation form the Summer Triangle. Identifying this enormous triangle is a quick way to orient yourself in the Northern Hemisphere's summer night's sky.

Cygnus is home to the giant stellar association Cygnus OB2, which contains the red supergiant star NML Cygni, one of the largest stars currently known. First discovered in 1964 during a rocket flight, Cygnus X-1 is a famous X-ray source, one of the strongest seen from Earth. It is thought to be a black hole with a mass 14.8 times that of the Sun, orbiting a blue supergiant star. At the other end of the electromagnetic spectrum, Cygnus A (3C 405) is one of the strongest radio sources in the sky. It is an active galaxy at a distance of 750 million light-years, and contains a supermassive black hole at its core with a mass that is 2 billion times that of the Sun.

VISUALIZATION

BOOST YOUR MINDSET

When you're feeling under stress and need to calm down and distance yourself from a situation, try this on-the-spot visualization.

To begin, find an image of a rainbow and focus on it for a couple of minutes. When you're ready, close your eyes and imagine you're sitting beneath the arch of the rainbow in your picture. You can feel the warmth of the sun on the top of your head, infusing you with peace.

With every breath in and out, the rainbow extends, its colours spreading and becoming more vibrant. Continue to breathe deeply, and picture the rainbow gradually descending from the sky, until it's touching your head. Slowly it wraps around you, covering you from head to toe in an array of vivid hues. You are drenched in all the colours of the rainbow. When you inhale, you take in the uplifting energy of each ray. As you exhale you release all the fear, worry and stress back into the air.

When you are ready, emerge from the rainbow, give your limbs a shake and do a mental check of your body. You should feel light, centred and relaxed.

Slow,
deep breathing
calms the body
and the mind, and is
particularly powerful
when coupled with a
visualization using
colour and light.

RAINBOW RISING

You are standing in a deep valley between a cluster of giant hills, mounds of earth that penetrate the grey sky. You have been walking, the stark silence of nature your only companion. The sky is a darkening smudge above your head. The grass beneath your feet is wet and it feels as if you're standing in thick clay. You twist around, in an attempt to take in the view from all sides. Emptiness greets you. There are slopes that rise and fall in every direction, just as your breath rises and falls. You are at one with the landscape, as much a part of it as the cluster of crows sweeping above your head.

The black plume of corvids softly caws, and it feels like they're speaking directly to you, trying to attract your attention in some way. The sound gets louder, more frantic and you reach up towards them, watch as they flounce higher into the air, heading for the hill's peak. The charcoal grey of the sky is a gaping hole, offering space and tranquillity and you drink in the sight of it. It has been raining, but the sun is out now, bursting through the clouds and chasing away the last of the gloom.

You smile.

Even the darkest skies can't keep the sun at bay.

Looking up, you notice intricate carvings, indents into the side of the bank and slithers of stone that jut from the earth. Birds gather upon these makeshift ledges; flitting from one to the other in an aerial dance. They peer down at you and suddenly you long to be up there with them, to experience their realm. Above this pinnacle a rainbow forms, it's an explosion of colour and made even brighter by the fact there are two of them. You clap your hands together and make a wish at this heavenly sight.

For a moment, it feels like the world is frozen. Time stands still and there is only you and the rainbow cascading down at your feet. Glittering hues swirl around you, like a glorious tornado and you feel yourself being lifted into the air. Carried by ribbons of light, you relax into the spectrum of colour.

Your arms and shoulders feel free from tension.

The muscles in your legs melt away to nothing, and your spine extends and softens.

You breathe deeply.

Your eyelids lower and you relax your neck and throat.

The ligaments in your body feel more fluid, as you continue to
float upwards.

It's as if you've become at one with the sky that surrounds you. You are a
spiritual being made up of particles of light, happy to be carried wherever
the rainbow takes you.

You close your eyes completely now and enjoy feeling as if you're made
of air. A smile curves your lips. There is no room for stress here. No room
for anything except joy. You drop your weight into your lower legs and
find that you are perfectly balanced. The wind supports you, holding
you upright as you float. As you open your eyes once more you see that
you are surfing the rainbow, gliding gracefully along its colourful edges.
Bathed in the light from each hue, you feel the colours seeping into your
aura. With every long, slow breath in you drink down each shade, taking
it deep into your soul. You sigh.

Relaxation sweeps over you as the colours resonate within.

All thoughts of the day ahead have gone. There is no pressure to do anything. You can simply be. The colours drape around you. They cocoon you in their brightness. The rainbow is never-ending; a bridge in the sky to a new way of being, a new, more relaxed you. The landscape moves beneath you, and although you are still a part of it, you feel removed, able to carry a sense of calm through your day.

The distance between the earth and the sky is like the distance you now feel from the things which cause you tension. Stretching your arms out at your sides, you let the breeze buffet you, and imagine for a second that you have wings that can lift you up, anytime, anywhere. The rainbow dips, and you begin to slide back down to Earth. It is a gradual motion, and you land delicately, as if you've never moved from the spot.

The smile is still upon your face and as you continue on your walk, you feel the rainbow, it entwines around you, bathing you in tranquillity. No matter where you are or what happens during your day, you will always hold serenity in your soul.

MIMICRY & MIMESIS

Biomimicry – design inspired by biological entities and processes –
is fundamentally a form of mindfulness. It is the tangible result of a
meditation upon nature, resulting in beautiful artefacts made through
natural mirroring. Biomimicry demands that we begin by closely studying
our natural environment. We can learn about more than just design by
looking at sealife. The sea turtle is a great example. Sea turtles have
existed for more than 100 million years; they are unrivalled ocean
travellers, swimming over epic distances. Green sea turtles can stay
under water for five hours, slowing their heart rate to as little as one
beat every nine minutes to conserve oxygen. This provides a lesson in
mindfulness – imagine what it is like to breathe as slowly as a sea turtle.

There are also powerful lessons to be learned from sealife about adaptation to circumstance. We humans often work against currents and winds, powering machines to journey in straight lines. This is hugely inefficient. Sea turtles drift along the current to travel. Mindfulness entails working with the given flow. Lao Tzu said: 'Conquering others takes force, conquering yourself is true strength.' We can expand this: conquering yourself is good; learning to respond and collaborate with others and our environment brings a shared strength beyond illusory divisions of self and other, humankind and nature. Biomimicry is such collaboration in action.

We arrive at a timeless truth: all living things are interconnected and interdependent. All life is linked to water and the creatures that live within it. The more we educate ourselves about sealife and the issues facing this ecosystem, the more we will want to help ensure its health and to cultivate mindfulness on behalf of the planet by tending the oceans.

PLANT PROCESSES

Have you ever wondered how a tree produces the energy to grow so big? Or how plants absorb water into their roots and what happens to it? Well, it is all down to a number of baffling invisible processes and actions.

PHOTOSYNTHESIS

A leaf is like a mini solar panel that captures radiant energy in chloroplast cells that contain chlorophyll (the green pigment involved in photosynthesis). The radiant energy, along with inhaled carbon dioxide and water, is converted into sugar and transported around the plant via the phloem (tissues). During photosynthesis the plant exhales oxygen as a by-product.

RESPIRATION

At night when the plant cannot photosynthesize, it respires carbon dioxide using the sugars or carbohydrates already stored within the plants to help it grow.

TRANSPIRATION

Plants emit water into the atmosphere through tiny pores in the underside of their leaves (stomata), which cools the air whilst also creating a tension that pulls water upward from the roots.

OSMOSIS

Water and nutrients enter the plant through its roots by passing through a semi-permeable membrane until the concentration on either side of the membrane is equal, namely - the moisture content in the root is the same as the soil.

All these processes are vital for the plant's survival. Without water for osmosis the stem will collapse and won't be able to transport water and food to the plant, the leaves will wither and won't be able to photosynthesize or transpire, which will further prevent the pull of water from the roots.

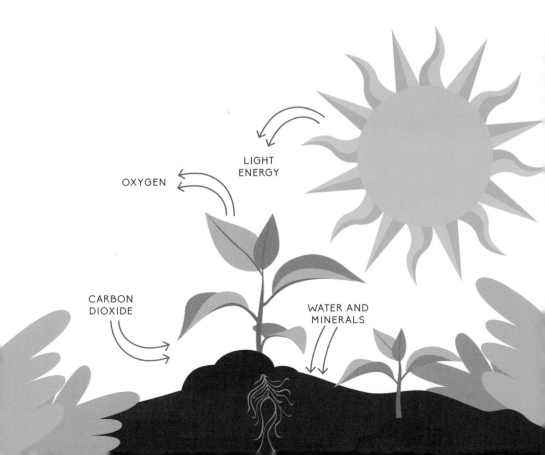

LIGHT ENERGY

OXYGEN

CARBON DIOXIDE

WATER AND MINERALS

SUNFLOWER
Helianthus annuus

Native to the Americas, sunflowers were originally cultivated by Native Americans for their nutritious seeds. A member of the Asteraceae family along with all other daisy flowers, this annual plant is well-loved for its sunshine-like flowers. October is the ideal time to harvest the seeds.

STEMS Rough, hairy woody.

LEAVES Broad, coarsely toothed, rough and growing alternately up the stem, getting smaller the higher up they grow. The leaves at the base of the plant are arranged opposite. The leaves have serrated edges, are 10–30 cm/4–12 inches long and range from triangular to heart-shaped, they have hairs on the upper and underside.

FLOWERS The flower heads consist of numerous small individual five-petaled florets. The outer flowers resemble petals and are called ray flowers. Sunflowers are Hermaphrodite. The flowers in the centre of the head are called disk flowers and are arranged in a spiral, they mature into seeds.

SEEDS Ripen September–October.

LAUNCH SEEDBOMBS Early spring in pots and mid-spring in situ.

GERMINATION TIME 14 days

HARVESTING SEEDS The seeds are ripe when the flower heads start to dry and turn to face the ground. Cut off flower heads keeping 20 cm/7¾ inches of the stem attached and hang them upside down inside a pillow case. After a few days you can rub the seeds out gently with your hand or a brush, or if you have two seed heads try rubbing them together.

PLANT CARE Grow in full sun, in fertile, moist but well-drained soil, pH 5.7–8.5. Sunflowers are happy in dry, poor to average soil and need little water or fertilizer.

PESTS AND DISEASES Banded sunflower moth, cutworm, slugs, snails, downy mildew, powdery mildew, rust.

CULINARY AND MEDICINAL USES The seeds have a delicious nut-like flavour and are rich in fats so can be made into oil or butter or ground up and used in baking. The sprouted seeds can be eaten raw. A tea made from the leaves is thought to be useful as an astringent, diuretic or expectorant.

AUTUMN

SEPTEMBER

OCTOBER

NOVEMBER

SEPTEMBER

Time to be mindful. Read, write, listen and reflect whilst outside in parks, fields or gardens.

WHO FOLLOWS?

There can be no more iconic image of autumn, in some parts of the world, than the sight of a flock of seagulls following the plough. The farmer turns the soil to sow the seed and the gulls flock behind the tractor to eat the worms and bugs, a moving tableau crossing the field back and forth. Birds left behind fly forwards to take their place at the front, their turn for the freshest pickings – a rolling cloud of excitement.

A similar sight is to be seen at sea, as a swirling cloud of seabirds scream with anticipation in the wake of a fishing trawler, waiting for the nets to be hauled in, for the catch to be sorted, unwanted fish discarded overboard. When we witness such scenes we experience a real sense of being part of the living ecosystem.

We share the world with other creatures; the seagulls belong to the present moment as much as we do.

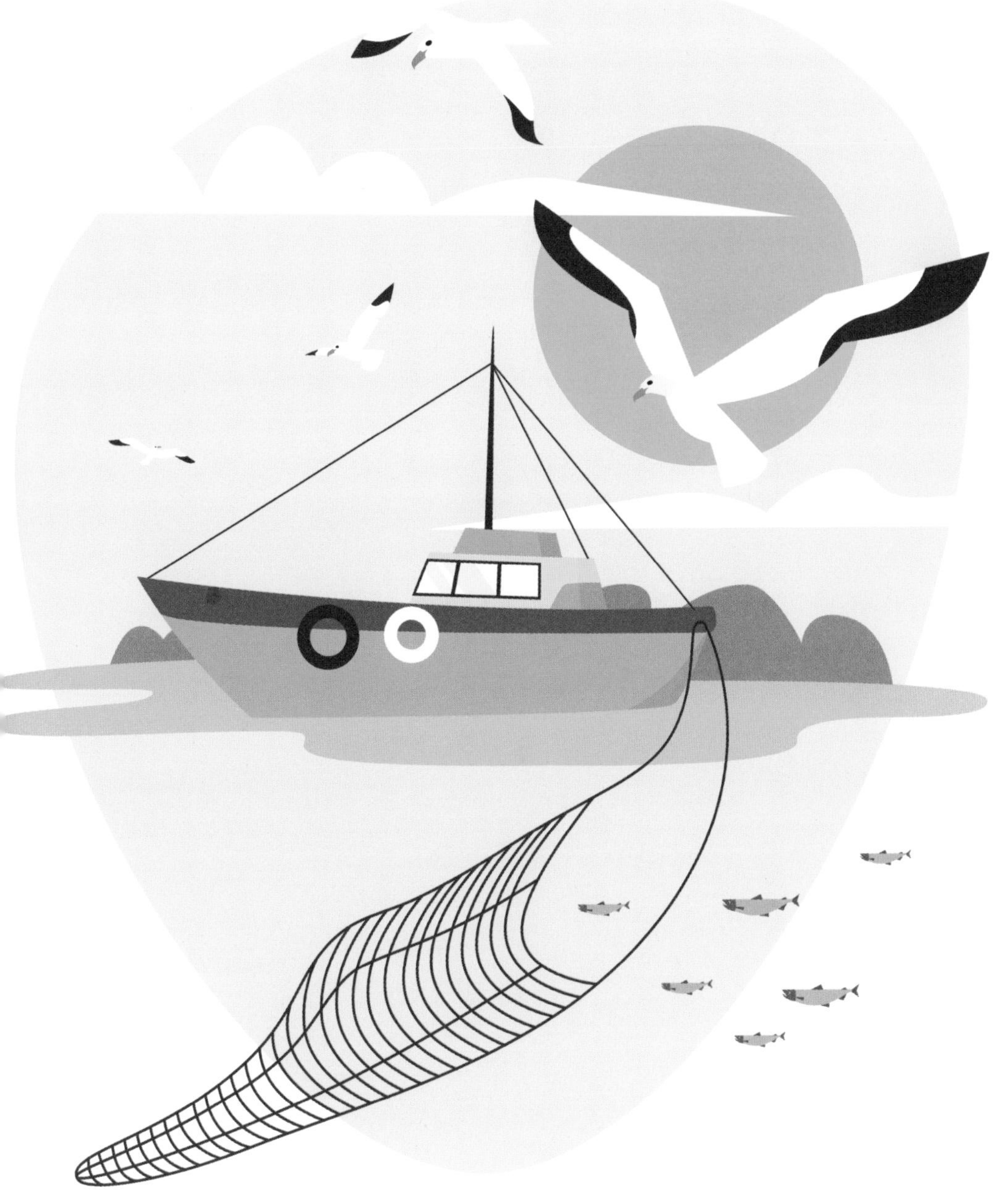

POTATOES
Solanum tuberosum

Growing potatoes is easy and loads of fun. Burrowing through the soil to find the tubers is like looking for buried treasure. They do take up a lot of space, however, so one option is to grow only early potatoes that are in the ground for less time than a main crop of potatoes.

PLANTING TIPS

Potatoes prefer plenty of sun, and they are heavy feeders, so either plant after your fertility-building phase of rotation or add well-rotted compost and manure before planting.

You'll be planting 'seed' potatoes, which look like normal potatoes, but they have eyes and come from a specialty garden centre certified free of disease. For an earlier crop, place the seed potatoes on a tray lined with newspaper and put somewhere to dry and to let the eyes shoot.

When the shoots are 2 cm/1 inch long, the potatoes are ready to be planted 8–15 cm/3–6 inches deep, in rows 50–75 cm/20–30 inches apart.

CULTIVATION

The young shoots of early crops may need protecting from night frost with a floating row cover, which can be removed once the weather warms up. Unless the weather is dry, you shouldn't need to water until new tubers start to form, which is usually about the same time that the plants begin to flower. Potato tubers exposed to light will turn green and become poisonous. To prevent this, take some of the soil from between the rows and hill it up in a ridge over the emerging shoots to cover the tubers. There are a few pests and diseases to watch out for: late summer blight is the worst, and it can be avoided by growing only early cultivars that are harvested before blight can take hold.

TIP
*Choose a
container at least
60 cm/2 feet deep. When
planting, leave enough room in
the top of the container so that
an extra 10 cm/4 inches of soil
can be added when the new
stems are 15 cm/
6 inches tall.*

WEED CONTROL

Potatoes are great at smothering weeds, but they do take time to get
going. The traditional process of hilling them is also a good way of
keeping them weeded at an early stage, and it helps to warm up the soil
on the ridge.

HARVEST

When the leaves begin to die down, or soon after flowers appear, your
potatoes are ready to harvest. Keep later cultivars intended for storing
in the ground for a few weeks so that the skin hardens. Scrape the skin
lightly with your nail to test; if you don't leave a mark, they are ready to
dig. Early cultivars are not suitable for storing.

> **GROW IN** Any rich and fertile, well-drained soil
>
> **PLANT** Throughout Spring before last frost
>
> **HARVEST** From late summer to the middle of Autumn
>
> **EAT** Fresh, or store in a cool, dry place for up to two weeks

FORAGING

HERBS

Foraging, or wildcrafting, is increasingly popular, and you need not live in the woods to do it. It's amazing how many useful herbs grow in the nooks and crannies of a city. When gathering from the wild, there are a few important considerations.

First, treat the environment with respect and don't overforage. A good guideline is to always take a little under half of what is there – and if the plant is endangered, don't take any at all. If you are gathering the root of a plant, or a whole plant (as opposed to just some flowers, leaves, stems or bark), then plant some seeds or a new plant. With some plants, you can divide the roots and replant half again.

Second, check for contamination. In farming areas, avoid land that has been crop sprayed, especially recently. In cities, find out the previous use of waste land, making sure it wasn't used for toxic chemical production, dumping, or such like. It's also important to be careful that you are not trespassing on private land, and make sure to check local laws about gathering plants.

Plant identification is an invaluable skill, and there are excellent books with clear photographs to help the lone learner. If you take this route, you must be extremely careful not to use the wrong plant: if you're not sure, leave it alone. Whilst few plants are seriously poisonous, some can harm and even kill you if taken by mistake. Before you pick, you could follow the native tradition of asking the plant's permission in your heart (respecting a 'no' if you feel you hear one), and offering gratitude and something in return. In North America, the traditional offering is tobacco; in Europe, it is oats or barley. Even if this seems strange to you, you may be surprised at the warmth it will bring you. The earth is a living treasury, and the more you recognize its offerings, the richer your life will be.

LEAVES

Leaves are elegantly crafted into many different shapes and sizes with the primary goal of harvesting light. They must be sheetlike, thin and translucent (to allow light to reach the innermost cells). They must have stalks, which may develop in an opposite or alternate pattern on the stem and elevate the leaves to positions where they can track the movement of the sun throughout the day.

There is an unlimited diversity in leaf characteristics. Some come in single blades or are divided into leaflets; some have leaf margins, which can be whole, toothed or wavy. All these characteristics are what botanists use to identify and describe a plant. Here are just some examples of leaf shapes and patterns found in nature. Why not go for a walk in a local park and see how many you can spot. Focus on the detail of the leaves you notice, appreciating the differences and similarities of each one.

OPPOSITE

ALTERNATE

PINNATE

DISSECTED

HEART-SHAPED

OBLIQUE

OBLANCEOLATE

LANCEOLATE

OBLONG

PALMATE

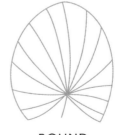

ROUND

MEDITATION
WAVE GOODBYE

The sun kisses your forehead as you lay upon the sand, it bathes you in adoration. This beach is what you deserve; a break from the everyday and some time to relax and reflect. Comforting rays brush against your skin whilst a gentle breeze ruffles your hair. You are alone, but not lonely. You hear the sounds of children playing, splashing in the sea. People in the distance talking and laughing, but they are getting further and further away with every breath, until they're just fragments, echoes drifting along the shoreline. The silence gives you perspective and your mind feels suddenly alert and ready for its next quest. Life is sweet and you are in a good place, a safe space. This is your version of paradise. In and out you breathe, in time with the ebb and flow of the ocean. On and on, in a continual loop, a cycle of rise and fall as you unwind. You can feel the stress falling from your shoulders, dissolving into the golden sand. Slowly you rise, until you're standing tall. Stretching up on your tip-toes, you imagine grasping the sun with both hands, pulling this fiery orb into your chest. You smile. All is good in your world right now.

Before you is the sea; a swell of vibrant sapphire with threads of emerald and the lightest aquamarine at the surface. A beautiful boundless beast, it moves in giant rolls and you wonder what it would be like to go with that flow. To surrender to the waves.

You walk forwards, your focus on the horizon. Deep azure blue washes over you. The shrill call of a sea bird captures your attention if only for a moment, then you are back, gaze fixed on the middle of the ocean, on the secrets beneath the watery brine. Your feet sink into the sand, swallowed by the glorious gold dust of those that went before you. The earth becomes moist, a clay-like substance that moulds to the shape of each foot. Still you move forwards fixed on your goal, on the cool trickle at the edge of the shore. You want to feel water lapping at your toes, hungrily seeking out each one in a bid to claim it. Soon you are there, paddling by the edge. Able to feel the refreshing nip of the water as you stroll along the beach.

The sun takes your breath away and you shield your eyes, as all the colours of the vista take on new life. Golds that veer towards amber catch your eye; palms the darkest green, they make you think of saturated rainforests, and the soft baby blue of the sky, an artist's palette painted to perfection. You sigh and let out any remaining stress. All worry is banished in this place. Calm is the only thing you feel.

You breathe in this moment. Finally, you understand that this is all you have. The present is a gift. You are ready to let go of the past. To release the pain you've been holding onto. You stop in your tracks. Turn to face the sea. Ever welcoming, it rushes towards you in the crest of a wave. You step back, making a mark with your toe. Then into the pliable sand you work, crafting a symbol to represent all of the hurt, guilt and fear that you feel. All of the things that have been holding you back. You make your mark upon the earth and pour all of those emotions into it. Then, when you are ready, you look towards the horizon once more.
'I give this to you,' you say. *'I release my pain. I let it all go.'*

The ocean smiles. Runs to greet you again. The waves eager to wash away the hurt and transform it into light. Smoothly and swiftly the sea heals, wiping the slate clean and stealing the symbol that you have made from the sand. In that one motion the pain is gone, swept away and you are left lighter, more radiant than you have ever been before. Your heart leaps, and suddenly you feel a pull to go deeper, to submerge in the watery depths and feel that healing energy surround you. Taking long strides, the waves part at your touch. The sea accepts you unconditionally. Within seconds you're up to the chest, arms sweeping, propelling you forwards. Your legs are floating behind you. There is little effort involved. The ocean carries and supports every movement you make.

Light as a feather, as a thought, as a breath.

You feel totally at peace. Healed from the inside out.

THE HEALING POWER OF WATER

Use the power of water to boost healing, by incorporating these top tips into your schedule.

Infuse body and soul with healing energy throughout the day by sipping water. This will keep you hydrated and also help you to remain focused in challenging situations. Imagine that each mouthful is imbued with positive energy, which surges through your body as you drink.

If you need an extra boost of vitality, run the cold tap and place your wrists underneath the flow of water for at least a minute. As you do this picture a stream of white light travelling up each arm and around your entire body. Breathe deeply and relax.

Alternatively fill the sink with cold water and submerge your hands. Close your eyes and imagine you are dipping your hands into the sea.

Running cold water on your wrists lowers the body's core temperature and heart rate and helps to reduce levels of cortisol, the stress hormone. This coupled with a relaxing visualization will make you feel instantly calmer.

All is good, all is calm.

I surrender to the
ebb and flow.

I release pain, I let it go.

Healing energy
washes over me.

RECIPE

HERBAL BATHS

Herbal baths cleanse the skin, as well as easing aches and pains. Put your chosen herbs in a small muslin bag hanging over the hot water tap as you fill the bath; they continue to infuse whilst you bathe. Therapeutic baths can be relaxing or invigorating – soak for 20 minutes for maximum effects.

RESTORATIVE BATHS

Make this citrus-scented bath blend for when your spirits need a pick-me-up and reminder of summer climes. Light a candle, set an intention to relax, and embrace your time for self-care.

3 TABLESPOONS FRESH LEMON BALM/MELISSA LEAVES

OR

3 TABLESPOONS FRESH SWEET MARJORAM LEAVES

TIP
*Try adding
60 ml/2 fl oz
full-cream or oat
milk to soften
the water.*

INVIGORATING BATHS

Energise your spirit and self with this refreshing botanical bath blend that will awaken all your senses – ready for fall and ready to embrace a fresh seasonal cycle.

3 TABLESPOONS FRESH HEATHER FLOWERING STEMS

OR

3 TABLESPOONS FRESH SAGE LEAVES

ECHINACEA (CONEFLOWER)
Echinacea purpurea

Echinacea was used by the Native Americans and the early settlers adopted it as a medicine. It is a fast-growing, versatile herbaceous perennial with a vigorous, long flowering season. It requires little attention once established and is an important foodplant for wildlife.

LEAVES Pale to dark green, coarse, toothed and hairy with three prominent veins.

STEMS Stoutly round, upright fuzzy stems bear opposite medium or large leaves at the base and intermittently along the stem, almost up to the flower head.

FLOWERS Hermaphrodite, sweet-scented pink, lavender or deep purple daisy-like ray flowers. The petals are 'reflexed' (point downwards) and surround a raised central orange or rich ochre cone.

SEEDS The seed head is dome-shaped, dense and prickly and the seeds are achenes – light brown, 5 mm/¼ inches long and cone-shaped with ragged toothed ends.

HARVESTING SEEDS Because the stems are so tough echinacea doesn't require staking. It copes well with adverse weather conditions. Cut back stems as the blooms fade to encourage further flower production. Cut back dead flower stems to the ground in autumn and feed in the spring or autumn. Water regularly, however, echinacea cannot tolerate being waterlogged. Divide the plant in spring or autumn and whilst you are at it you could take some root cuttings.

CULINARY AND MEDICINAL USES Echinacea is commonly used to prevent colds and boost the immune system. It comes in many forms such as tonics, teas, tinctures, tablets, lotions and ointments, root powder and in loose, dry leaf and flower form. For tea, place two teaspoons of dried or fresh leaves in a teapot and cover with one cup of boiling water. Leave to steep for 20 minutes, strain and enjoy. Historically, a very important herbal plant, which is still widely used to help alleviate a variety of ailments such as skin rashes, gynaecological problems, toothache, sore throats and colds and to boost the immune system; it may also help speed up recovery time after an infection.

HEIGHT/SPREAD 120 x 45 cm/47 x 18 inches

HABITAT Gravelly hillsides, open woodland, cultivated beds

THRIVES IN Full sun or partial shade (suffers in deep shade)

SOIL Drought tolerant; grows on most moist, free-draining soils; tolerates clay

LIFESPAN Hardy perennial herb

FLOWERS June–September

FORM Clump-forming, rhizomatous, upright stems

LEAF FORM Lanceolate to ovate

POLLINATED BY Insects

CAPTURING SUNLIGHT

All food growing relies eventually on the sun – plants capture sunlight and use it to make sugars from water and carbon dioxide. The more of that sunlight you can grab, the more food you can grow. Sunlight that hits bare soil and is reflected back up into the atmosphere is wasted.

Many of the inputs used to help plants grow are based on sunlight. Man-made nitrogen fertilizers rely on oil and gas made from plants over the millennia. Animal manures also derive originally from sunlight, because animals eat plants, which need sunlight, and excrete the manure for us to use to feed our garden. The more of the current sunlight you can capture, the less you rely on using the world's bank of stored energy like gas and oil.

A core principle of organic gardening is to keep the soil covered for as much of the year as possible. The ideal is to have a plant growing at all times to capture energy, however, it is not always possible to have a food crop growing so you can also use other plants to fit into your garden to help.

OCTOBER

Time to be earthy. Nurturing your garden is the best way to grow and thrive the soul.

MYCELIUM

Above ground, you spy a mushroom. A shelf fungus poking out from a dying tree; a stinkhorn triumphantly bursting from the mulch; a fairy circle of gently domed lawn mushrooms speaking of rainy days. What you do not see is the larger part of the fungi, the net of white feathery strands below ground, called mycelium. You have seen mycelium if you've ever kicked apart a decaying log. They look like nerve cells or slow, soft lightning pushing their way through decaying matter. Mycelium doesn't just work to break down organic matter, however; it acts as a living internet connecting plants below ground. Through the mycelium, plants literally communicate with each other. Hairs on plant roots touch mycelium strands, enabling the transfer of carbon, nitrogen, phosphorus and other chemicals through a forest or garden network. They exchange information through these chemicals, a process scientists are still studying.

The fungal networks also work to build the plants' immune systems by triggering chemicals that fight off insects and damaging fungi. In turn, the plants share these chemicals with other plants, through both their roots and their leaves, creating a symbiotic network that is much stronger than a single plant species can ever be.

This unseen (to us) network of chemicals, root capillaries and information is not unlike our own human networks. Not just the internet, to which plant communities have inevitably been compared, but also dynamic networks in everyday, molecular reality. We can use the image of networked mycelium to visualize the connections amongst those around us, both to our own species and with other beings. These connections are formed through actions, like helping a stranger carry their groceries, and through energy. Imagine each person as a point of light, sending our mycelium strands of energy out towards those around us. This living energetic network reaches not just through space, but through time. We are connected through strands of light to the past, the present and the future. We are connected to people, animals and plants.

A REWARDING EXISTENCE

Community action groups are making food accessible, nutritious and sustainable for neighbourhoods on full-scale city farms, roadside allotments and even waste ground. It is a refreshing alternative to our tendency to focus inwards as we strive to make ends meet and provide a decent lifestyle for our families, or ourselves. These pressures can be isolating, making life seem a lonely struggle. But in communal actions – whether sharing goods, knowledge, skills or space – we find a more social and rewarding way to exist. Hard outcomes aside, in the act of creating nutritionally rich food or bringing solar panels to housing estates, you can discover a sense of belonging and common purpose as you make change happen alongside neighbours you might otherwise ignore. Tilling the soil as you chat to a new friend two doors away, or helping to raise funds to rescue a local green space, gives us a chance to be with others who care about making our cities more pleasant. It also exposes us to a side of humanity easy to forget when our only interaction with the world is through the prism of news bulletins. Knowing that such caring, positive people live on your doorstep is a refreshing mental tonic.

FORAGED LEAF DISH

This one-of-a-kind trinket dish is a quick and easy way to spruce up your bedside table, and makes a fun craft activity for all ages. It's a perfect project for children during long school holidays, especially on rainy days – take a trip down to your nearest woodland and have a rummage for the perfect leaf! Combining nature and craft is bound to entertain small hands. If you enjoy making this dish, consider creating a variety of dishes using different-shaped leaves.

MAKES 1

TOOLS AND MATERIALS

- · 200 g/7 oz white air-drying clay
- · Scales
- · Rolling pin
- · Clean, dry leaf of choice
- · Scalpel
- · Cling film (plastic wrap)
- · Bowl or mould, at least 15 cm/6 inches in diameter
- · Fine sandpaper
- · Acrylic craft paints
- · Small dishes (for the paints)
- · Thin and medium acrylic paintbrushes
- · Clear water-based varnish
- · Medium paintbrush for varnishing

METHOD

1. Cover your work surface, and weigh out 200 g/7 oz of white air-drying clay. Roll out your clay so that it is 5 mm/¼ inch thick all over and 20 x 15 cm/ 8 x 6 inches in size – large enough for a leaf that is approximately 13 x 13 cm/ 5 x 5 inches.

2. Place your clean, dry leaf face down on your clay. Roll your rolling pin over the leaf a few times, applying medium pressure so that the leaf sticks to the clay.

3. Using a scalpel, cut around the leaf, leaving a 0.5–1-cm/ ¼–½-inch border of clay all the way around.

4. Smooth any rough edges of the clay with your finger and a dab of water.

5. Place a piece of cling film (plastic wrap) inside your chosen bowl or mould. This will stop your clay from sticking to the bowl whilst it dries. Gently press your clay leaf shape into the bottom of the bowl. This will give your leaf dish its curved shape. Leave to dry for 24 hours.

6. Once the clay leaf is dry, gently remove it from the bowl and peel off the real leaf to reveal the pattern underneath.

TO FINISH

1. You can either leave your leaf dish plain or add some detail to the marks that were left behind by the leaf. Before you apply any paint, smooth any rough edges using fine sandpaper.

2. Prepare your acrylic paint. Pour a small amount into a small dish and water it down a little.

3. Use a medium paintbrush to apply a layer of paint within the border of the leaf. When the background is dry to the touch, apply details along the veins of the leaf using a thin paintbrush. You can add as much or as little detail as you like. Leave to dry for 4 hours.

4. Once the paint is dry, apply a layer of varnish to the top of your dish, using a medium-sized clean paintbrush. Leave to dry for 24 hours, then turn over and coat the bottom of the dish. Leave to dry for another 24 hours.

PUMPKIN
Cucurbita

The golden rule for a zero-waste pumpkin is to make sure you grow a tasty variety. Many of those grown for lanterns have a watery, disappointing flavour. Choose for taste and you can eat well and still make your lantern for Halloween.

GROWING TIPS

- Grow quick crops like spring onion or salad around the plant when they are young and harvest them as the pumpkins grow to fill the space.
- Grow the pumpkins amongst taller plants like runner beans and sweetcorn.

SEEDS

You can eat pumpkin seeds, but there is a catch. Varieties have been specially bred to have seeds with a soft coat that don't need shelling. The flesh from these types is not very good to eat, it is usually pretty tasteless and stringy. The seeds from most eating pumpkins have a shell that is edible but pretty crunchy. You can roast them with oil, salt and spices, though, and it's pretty good, but you need a good set of teeth.

FLOWERS

You can eat pumpkin flowers. Raw in salads, or stuffed and baked, or even deep fried. Pick male or female flowers, though make sure you have let some fruit set first. Some varieties can be bitter, so check one before serving them all up to your friends.

TIP

*Pumpkin plants
do better if sown directly so
long as the soil is warm enough
18°C/65°F and it's at least 100 days
before the first frosts come in the autumn.
For those with shorter, colder summers you
can sow into pots indoors in the heat and
then plant out after the last spring frost.
Make sure you protect from the wind as
they are susceptible to damage for
the first couple of weeks.*

HARVEST

Pumpkins are ready when you are able to gently press your fingernail into the skin of the pumpkin without leaving a mark.

YIELD

Pumpkins need a surprising amount of space. The largest varieties will need 29.5 x 29.5 cm/11 x 11 inches for each plant. Mini varieties such as, Jack Be Little, can manage with 19.5 x 19.5 cm/7 x 7 inches.

SOW Spring indoors or very early summer outdoors

PLANT Early summer

HARVEST Autumn

EAT Fresh, from autumn for 2–5 months

PUMPKIN PICKLE

Preserving food is the gift that keeps on giving. You can make salads in the depths of winter with the dark green of iron-filled spinach, the crunch of roasted pumpkin seeds and the tang of this pumpkin preserve. If you are so inclined, add a bit of fresh cheese, a hard-boiled egg or some marinated tofu for extra protein. And when you do so, give thanks for the immunizing boost of vitamin A coming your way, the ancient knowledge to which you have reconnected, and the memory of your autumn ritual.

MAKES 1

INGREDIENTS

- 1 medium Hokkaido (or any other thick-skinned pumpkin or squash)
- 400 ml/13 fl oz apple cider vinegar
- 250 ml/8½ fl oz water
- 300 g/9 oz beet sugar
- 12 black peppercorns
- 8 whole cloves
- 2 bay leaves
- 1 crushed cinnamon stick

METHOD

1. Prep It: Cut the pumpkin in half, scoop out the insides, cut it into quarters and then peel off the skin. Cut the quarters into cubes. Pumpkin is a dense fruit and small pieces ensure that the brine will penetrate them completely.

2. Make It: In a medium pot, combine the vinegar, water and sugar. Stir the mixture until the sugar dissolves, then add the spices and cubed pumpkin. Bring to a boil and then reduce to a simmer for 30 minutes. Pumpkin should be almost fork tender, but not quite.

3. Preserve It: To store throughout the winter, place your pickle in a sterilized jar then boil the sealed jars so that the tops of the jars are covered by at least 2.5 cm/ 1 inch of water for 10–15 minutes. Remove from the water and let them cool completely before placing in your pantry. Let the flavour develop for at least one week before consumption.

4. Twist It: Get creative with the spices used – feel free to omit the cloves and cinnamon and throw in some thinly sliced onion and mustard seeds instead, or experiment with another concoction of your own.

LEAF COLOUR

Autumnal colour is a common feature of many temperate deciduous trees, and develops as the green pigments are broken down in the leaf.

Leaves contain other pigments, but these are mostly masked by the intense green of chlorophyll. They can often be seen, however, at the beginning and end of the seasons. Many trees have leaves that are bronze or red when they first emerge in spring or summer, and many are well-known for their striking autumn colours of yellow, red or purple.

These other pigments have several functions. In young foliage they may protect developing chloroplasts (structures that contain chlorophyll and where photosynthesis occurs) from intense radiation, which can damage them, as well as making the foliage less attractive to predators. In mature leaves, although the pigments may not be visible they can absorb excess radiation, which might otherwise overload the photosynthetic system.

The other leaf pigments usually break down after chlorophyll, so the green colour of the leaf disappears leaving its autumn colour, which is determined by the remaining pigments. When leaves of deciduous trees turn colour and fall in the autumn, they are not simply dying; they are being recycled by the tree because leaves contain a sizeable supply of nutrients, not least in the form of chlorophyll, which is rich in magnesium and nitrogen. That this is an active process can easily be seen by observing the fate of a branch broken on a tree in summer. In the autumn most of the tree's leaves will have changed colour and dropped whilst those on the broken branch remain attached and brown. Leaf shedding requires a considerable input of energy from the plan. It is thought that leaf pigments can protect chlorophyll from intense radiation, enabling it to remain active for as long as possible before the leaves are shed.

BERGAMOT/BEE BALM
Monarda

This clump-forming, easy-to-grow plant, which spreads by running underground stems, has dark green leaves and impressive shaggy blooms. It will flower continuously throughout the season if deadheaded periodically and makes a good companion plant because it attracts pollinators.

STEMS Square-stemmed, characteristic of the Lamiaceae family. They are upright, tough and covered in fine dense hairs.

LEAVES Leaves are dark green, oval-shaped and coarsely toothed with red leaf veins; they have fine hairs on the underside and on the topside are sparsely hairy.

FLOWERS The hermaphrodite, ragged-looking showy flower heads comprise about 30 long curving tubular flowers, 3–4 cm/1³/₁₆–1¹/₂ inch long, above reddish bracts. The flowers come in colours and shades ranging from red and mauve to white. The tubular shape of the flowers makes it easy for bees to fly in to feed from the sweet nectar and pollinate the plant in the process.

SEEDS As the seeds ripen, the seed pod dries and looks honeycomb-like and button-shaped. The nutlets (seeds) are held at the bottom of the calyx on a kind of pad and when they ripen they simply roll out and onto the ground. The tiny seeds are 1–2 mm/¹/₁₆ inch long, nut-shaped and a light brown colour. It is hard to separate them from the chaff because of their size so don't worry too much.

HARVESTING SEEDS The seeds heads are ripe and ready to harvest August–October.

PLANT CARE Cutting back hard after flowering encourages more blooms. Propagate by division in spring or autumn.

CULINARY AND MEDICINAL USES Steep the leaves in water to make a refreshing citrusy tea or add to normal tea. The young shoot tips, flowers and leaves can be used raw and added to salads as a garnish. The young shoots and leaves can be cooked to enhance the flavour of foods. Frequently used to aid in treating digestive disorders and sickness, and believed to act as a carminative for flatulent colic, an expectorant and a diuretic.

HEIGHT/SPREAD 90 x 40 cm/35 x 18 inches

HABITAT Roadsides, railways, waste ground, fields, woodland, cultivated beds

THRIVES IN Partial or deep shade

SOIL Grows on most soils but thrives on acid clay soils

LIFESPAN Hardy perennial herb

FLOWERS June–September

FORM Clump-forming

LEAF FORM Ovate, spear-shaped

POLLINATED BY Bees

GARDEN TASK LIST:
LATE SUMMER & AUTUMN

When summer starts to recede and autumn spreads its blanket over the ground, jobs become less urgent. However, there are still some that need to be done within a definite time frame. Fruit still needs picking, particularly soft fruit such as raspberries, which will need a regular harvest to prevent them from spoiling. If you use cover crops, sow them in plenty of time before it gets too cold.

Some tasks come under the category of 'do them now and they're easy; leave them until spring and they're not'. Some forward thinking and planning at the end of the year can save you time and heartache once the chaos of the new season starts.

GROUND PREPARATION

If you are mulching, autumn is a good time to cut back any growth from previous crops. Leave this debris on the surface and cover with plain cardboard or straw. This blocks out light and allows loose nutrients to be absorbed for later release. You can also add a thick layer of garden compost or well-rotted manure. The plant residues will die over the winter and hopefully give you easy-to-work soil the following spring.

SOWING & PLANTING

Late summer and early autumn is a good time to get a cover crop sown, when the preceding crop has finished, but don't forget those crops that like being out over winter, such as garlic, shallots and fava beans, which can all be planted in the autumn. Cover crops are useful over winter because they are great at mopping up any loose nutrients in the soil that might be otherwise lost to winter rains. They also protect the structure of the soil and add valuable organic matter to the ground when you dig them back in. For late sowing, try rye grasses or quick-maturing crops, such as mustard and phacelia.

SAVING SEEDS

Some plants will seed in late summer, but most come in to their own in autumn. Collect from open-pollinated varieties and make sure you harvest the seeds as dry as possible; you will probably need to dry them further in either a dry shed or warm room. Once dry, store them in a cool, dry place.

LOOKING AHEAD TO WINTER

Winter evenings are a time for planning and drawing up next year's rotations. In mild climates, winter is also a great time for giving fruit trees a formative prune, except for cherries, plums and other stone fruits, which need to be done in summer. Avoid pruning if a hard frost is forecast because the cold can cause damage to fresh wounds.

GRATITUDE MEDITATION

Gratitude can be a part of your daily mindfulness practice. Like following your breath or tuning into present sensation, it can be done in just a moment. These little moments add up, shifting your overall perspective to one of presence and joy. Gratitude can also be the focus of a longer, more deliberate meditation. Here is one you can practise in your garden.

Find a place in your garden to sit comfortably. Take several breaths, following the air as it is pulled into your chest and released. Feel the pressure of your sitting bones on the ground or chair beneath you as the Earth pulls you towards her. Feel the sensation of air on your skin. Open your eyes if they are closed, and let them rest gently on whatever is in front of you. What has that object brought you? Why is it in your life? Try not to get caught up in a story about this plant or garden structure, but let the reason and gift of this object simply arise in your mind. Is there a reason for gratitude for this item? Usually there is. Everything in the garden has a little bit of a story, from the plants to the mulch on the paths to the reclaimed boards of the raised beds. What are the stories of your garden? What connections have brought these items before you at this point in time and what gifts will they bring you? Now gently shift your attention to something else nearby. Let its story arise, and send it gratitude. Stay present to your body, your breath and the now as you glance gently about your garden, sending out thankfulness. Lastly, send your own self gratitude. Your body, heart and soul make this garden what it is. Notice how your energy has shifted simply by feeling gratitude.

NOVEMBER

Time to be curious. Notice the wildlife, fauna and flora that flourish all year round.

APPLE TREES
Malus pumila

Apples are probably the most common fruit tree to be planted in temperate areas, partly because they are easy to grow and produce well, and there is a huge number of delicious cultivars to choose from. Dwarf varieties can be grown in containers or small spaces.

PLANTING TIPS

To get the soil right before planting, dig the ground over and remove weeds, and then prepare a planting hole a bit deeper than the tree roots so that the graft union (where the rootstock meets the top growth, usually visible as a small bulge) is just above ground level. Water in well as you backfill and firm around the roots with your heel. Finally, add a mulch of aged compost around the tree.

CULTIVATION

Keep well-watered in the first year after planting, even if the weather is cool. Once established, trees on all but the smallest dwarf stock (or those in containers) should cope without watering. After a few years, trees need formative pruning in winter to create a healthy shape. Remove crossing or wayward branches and shorten new shoots by half or one-third to encourage production.

WEED CONTROL

It is vital to maintain a weed-free area in the root zone, at least for the first couple of years. Once established, the trees will be able to cope with some ground cover around the trunk.

HARVEST

Exact harvest times for each cultivar will vary from region to region and year to year. Either check regularly to see if the fruit comes off easily in your hand, or wait for the first fruit to drop and then harvest them all. Keep records to make life easier in future years.

LIFESPAN Many years

PLANT Bare-root plants are planted in late autumn or early spring

GROW IN Any fertile, well-drained soil

TIP
Use a dwarf tree for container growing, or else the tree will quickly become rootbound. Feed annually when the leaves begin to grow, and keep the soil just moist.

HOW THE AGE OF
A TREE IS CALCULATED

Early in the twentieth century an American astronomer, A.E. Douglass (1867–1962), invented the science of dendrochronology when he correctly predicted historic climate patterns (and solar activity) would be reflected in tree rings. He demonstrated how a damp, warm year will produce a wide ring, whilst a drought results in a very narrow band. Occasionally, a particularly bad summer means the growth ring is absent. In other words, the ring pattern is effectively a bar code and can be 'read' against a scientific database of tree cross sections. Scientists can tell how old a tree was when it was felled, and can even determine exactly when it was growing at any point over the past 26,000 years.

Growth rings are most easily viewed by taking a horizontal cross section through the trunk. This is possible with a fallen tree but not a method to contemplate with a prized veteran.

These bands are the result of each year's spurt of new growth. The inner, lighter ring is formed in spring when growth is comparatively rapid. The outer part, or 'summer wood', is denser and darker because it is produced more slowly.

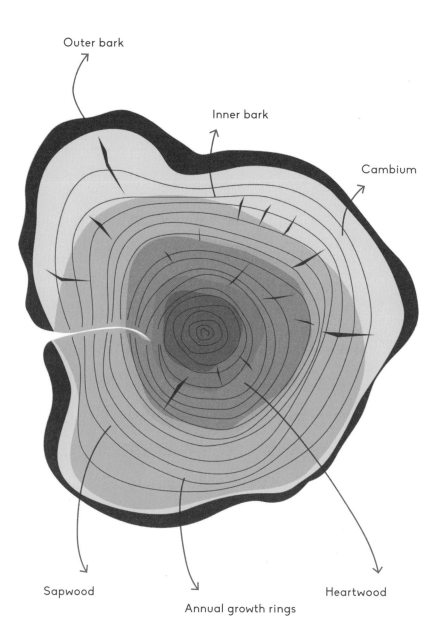

Outer bark

Inner bark

Cambium

Sapwood

Annual growth rings

Heartwood

ROSEHIP, HAWTHORN & PINE THROAT LOZENGES

Nature's kingdom is abundant in tall sorts of powerful remedies for injuries, emergencies and life's ups and downs. This recipe uses the best of the hedgerow larder to create a batch of soothing lozenges that are guaranteed to relieve even the sorest throat.

MAKES ROUGHLY 100 SWEETS

INGREDIENTS

- 3 generous handfuls of fresh rosehips
- 2 generous handfuls of fresh hawthorn berries
- up to around 500g/2½ cups of sugar
- up to around 500g/1½ cups of golden syrup
- 50ml/3 tbsp + 1 tsp pine tincture
- 20 drops lemon essential oil

METHOD

1. Collect your berries, and immediately cover with boiling water. Leave to cool.

2. Mash up the mixture a little, then strain through a double layer of muslin.

3. Mix this liquid (about 400ml/10 cups) with equal amounts of both sugar and golden syrup.

4. Make into sweets stirring in the pine tincture and lemon essential oil just before pouring the mixture into a set of sweet moulds. Leave to set for 24 hours before using.

THE PLEIADES CLUSTER

Taurus, one of the Zodiac constellations, is a large, prominent fixture in the later part of the year. Within the area of the constellation is the Pleiades cluster, or 'Seven Sisters' (M45), best viewed in November of each year. Despite the name, there are actually six stars visible to the naked eye, and if you look through binoculars or a telescope you'll find hundreds of stars sparkling like diamonds.

FINDING AWE & BEAUTY

Gazing up at the sky on a really dark night is mesmerizing: pitch dark from horizon to horizon, punctuated by thousands of points of twinkling lights, like tiny jewels on a silk cloth. And when you see something like the Pleiades in a telescope for the first time, you can't fail to be awestruck. Whether we know the science behind what we're looking at or not, the intrinsic beauty of the night sky remains unchanged. It's a source of inspiration, fascination and wonder. The next time you look up, take a moment to allow the exquisite splendour of the starscape to capture your eyes and your heart.

RECONNECTING WITH THE WORLD

There are countless small signs that signify our place in the year and link us to the seasons. The scream of the new season's birds as they fly high, performing dramatic loop-the-loops as they catch insects on the wing, back from their long migration. Sitting inside an artificially lit room, we can be surprised to find we have lost track of the time of day. Reconnecting with the natural world is reassuring and calms the soul. The knowledge that deep down the earth is still turning, the seasons are changing and all is well with the world – this provides security and helps to put into perspective our own often minor aggravations and inconveniences that grow to dominate our lives.

Gardening brings us both into the moment and into our ancient past. A holistic approach to gardening includes not only knowledge of planting dates and soil microbes but also of your own sense of wellness as the gardener. It's all interconnected, like plant roots beneath the soil. We each grow in our own time.

AN APPRECIATION OF LEAVES

In spite of their importance to life, their abundance, and their presence over a large proportion of the year, leaves are perhaps the least appreciated part of a tree. We often talk of beautiful flowers or wonderful bark, but leaves are generally accorded a mention only for their brief, but often spectacular, autumn colours.

Leaves are all around us, we see them every day, but do we really look at them? To many of us, a leaf is just that, a leaf, but the leaf of every species is different in one way or another – not only in the shape, but in many other respects, too. In some cases the differences may be small, but noticing them is just a matter of training the eye.

The first thing to do when identifying a tree is to turn a leaf over, since the lower surface holds most clues as to its identity. First-hand knowledge of what the leaf feels like and how it smells can be recalled when the tree is seen again. These features help us to put together a 'character' for each tree, which might also include such things as how its leaves are held and how they reflect the light. We are all very good at recognizing very small facial differences, and the same process can be applied to trees and leaves.

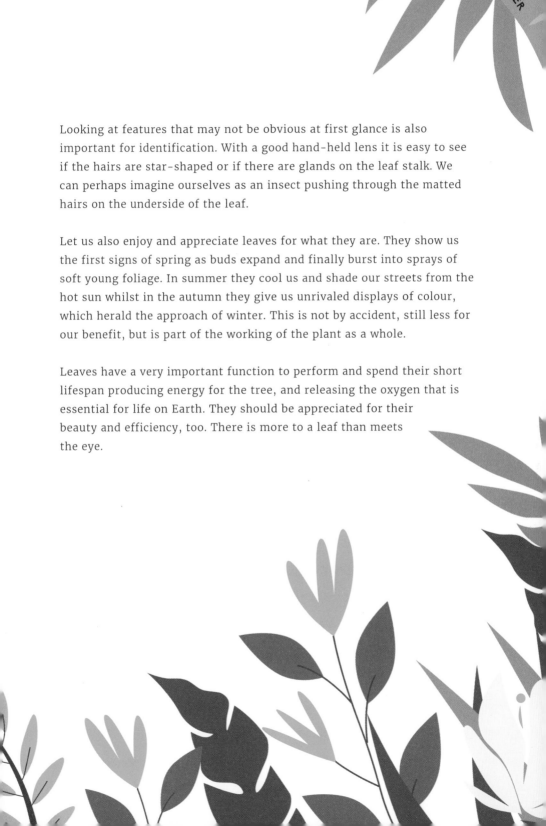

Looking at features that may not be obvious at first glance is also important for identification. With a good hand-held lens it is easy to see if the hairs are star-shaped or if there are glands on the leaf stalk. We can perhaps imagine ourselves as an insect pushing through the matted hairs on the underside of the leaf.

Let us also enjoy and appreciate leaves for what they are. They show us the first signs of spring as buds expand and finally burst into sprays of soft young foliage. In summer they cool us and shade our streets from the hot sun whilst in the autumn they give us unrivaled displays of colour, which herald the approach of winter. This is not by accident, still less for our benefit, but is part of the working of the plant as a whole.

Leaves have a very important function to perform and spend their short lifespan producing energy for the tree, and releasing the oxygen that is essential for life on Earth. They should be appreciated for their beauty and efficiency, too. There is more to a leaf than meets the eye.

VARNISH TREE
Toxicodendron vernicifluum

The Varnish Tree, which is also known as the Lacquer Tree, is a deciduous tree with a broadly columnar habit. It bears its small yellow-green flowers in late spring to early summer. It is cultivated for its sap, which is used to produce the lacquer used in Chinese and Japanese lacquerware. There is some evidence that the Japanese trees were introduced several thousand years ago from China, for their durable timber and sap.

LEAF TYPE Pinnate

LEAF SHAPE Oblong in outline

LEAF SIZE 35 x 20 cm/14 x 8 inches

ARRANGEMENT Alternate

BARK Dark gray, fissured with age

FLOWERS Small and yellowish green, in large axillary panicles to 30 cm/12 inches long

FRUIT A small, resinous, bluish white drupe about 7 mm/ ¼ inch across in large pendulous clusters

DISTRIBUTION East Asia and India

HABITAT Forests on hills and mountains

The leaves of the
Varnish Tree are pinnate
and up to 35 cm/14 inches long
and 20 cm/18 inches across. They
are composed of up to 13 untoothed
leaflets that are ovate to oblong, and
up to 13 cm/5 inches long and 6 cm/21^1/2
inches across. Borne on a short, downy
stalk, they are smooth or nearly so
above, and covered in yellow-gray
hairs beneath.

BREATHE WITH NATURE

Some of the pleasure of walking in a forest is the way it demands that you look about you in every direction, peering up, down, around and deep into its depths—not because it is scary, but because it is a three-dimensional experience. The canopy above your head is as interesting as the ground beneath your feet; the undergrowth and ferns close by the path are as eye-catching as the trunks of the trees. Stands of straight timber, like the pillars of a great cathedral, reveal intriguing caverns of space—dark and mysterious. The walker can't help looking between and beyond the brush, the branches and the trunks, probing the half-light and the shadows.

One instinctively walks slowly through a wood or forest, as though venturing on to hallowed ground. There is so much to take in, the senses alerted from every direction – the smell of loam and rotting leaves, the noisy clatter of a wood pigeon flying off, the crackle of broken twigs as some startled creature, glimpsed for a moment in the dappled light, disappears into the dense undergrowth.

Find a place to stop. Get intimate. Feel the texture of a tree trunk, the smooth flanks of a beech or the rough, spongy and punchable bark of a redwood. Breathe deeply and inhale the smell of the humus on the forest floor. If possible, find a place to sit, a log perhaps, or if you are lucky and you are walking the forest path in a park, there may be a bench. This would be a good spot to do a mindful breathing exercise. Take time. Recognize any distracting or troubling thoughts you may have; acknowledge them and let them go. Focus on the air as you inhale slowly, opening your lungs then exhaling without effort. Become aware of yourself as a breathing body sitting amongst trees.

LETTING GO

It's usually easy for a gardener to clear away old leaves, stalks and rotten fruit from the garden. We know that clearing spent plant matter reduces the risk of undesirable fungal infections, insects and vermin. We toss the old matter onto the compost to be transformed into nourishing new soil. Clearing accumulated stuff from other areas of our homes, however, is often harder for us to do. This may include things and situations both. What do you need to release from your life?

Let the energy of the garden guide you. Just as you get rid of old plant matter to prepare for the next season, let yourself release old things. Write in your garden journal about how letting go frightens you, and also how doing so will make space for new growth in your life.

What do you need to release and let go?

What is keeping you from doing so?

NATURE KNOWLEDGE

By following a few simple maintenance procedures, you will give your plants the best chance of remaining healthy and vigorous and help to avoid attack from pests and diseases. You should act immediately upon any signs of pest damage or disease and take professional advice if necessary.

DEADHEADING

A flower's primary goal is to set seed. If you constantly cut off the dead heads the plant goes into overdrive, sending out more flowers in an effort to reproduce.

PRUNING

Cutting back dead, damaged or diseased parts of the plant encourages growth and helps maintain vigour. Do this in spring or autumn and either compost the prunings or, if diseased, destroy them on a fire (use the ashes to condition the soil with potassium).

DIVISION

To divide an overgrown plant, dig it up, remove as much of the soil from the roots as you can, and cut the plant in half with a sharp knife. Replant the parent plant in the original hole and the new plant in a new position. Water thoroughly before and after planting until established.

ROOT CUTTINGS

Take a healthy stout root, cut it into 5 cm/2 inch sections and pot it in well-drained compost with the tip of the cutting just shy of the top of the soil. Do not overwater your cuttings. Shoots should emerge in early spring.

AIR CIRCULATION

Plants need good air circulation to help release waste gases and reduce the chances of disease and attack. Space plants according to size, which aids circulation and prevents competing for nutrients and soil water.

WINTER

DECEMBER

JANUARY

FEBRUARY

DECEMBER

Time to be connected. Embrace nature's cycles and weather in all its enlightening forms.

MOUNTAIN HOLLY
Ilex montana

The Mountain Holly, also known as the Mountain Winterberry, is a deciduous large shrub or small tree of spreading habit with smooth shoots, often shrubby with several stems from the base. The bright red fruits are amongst the largest of the American hollies, and can persist well into winter. They are attractive to birds, which disperse the seeds. It is occasionally grown in gardens and thrives best in woodland conditions.

LEAF TYPE Simple

LEAF SHAPE Broadly elliptic to ovate

LEAF SIZE 9 x 5 cm/3½ x 2 inches

ARRANGEMENT Alternate

BARK Smooth and grey, with prominent lenticels

FLOWERS Small and white, in clusters in the leaf axils; males and females on separate plants

FRUIT A spherical red berry 1 cm/½ inch across

HABITAT Moist woods in the mountains

The leaves of the
Mountain Holly are rather
thin in texture, broadly elliptic to
ovate, up to 9 cm/3½ inches long and
5 cm/2 inches across. They are tapered at
the base to a petiole of about
1.5 cm/⅝ inches, and taper-pointed at
the tip with a sharply toothed margin.
Dark green above and paler beneath,
they are smooth on both sides
or havewhite hairs along
the veins.

RAINWATER HARVESTING

Water is our most precious resource, and in this current climate it is essential that gardeners and farmers harvest their own water. Recycling rainwater is cheap and environmentally friendly and your plants prefer it because, unlike most domestic tap water, it hasn't been treated with chemicals.

You can harvest rainwater from the house or shed roof by rigging up gutters or you can capture water from existing gutters by intercepting the drainage pipes and guiding them into a water tank. Systems can be purchased in gardening shops or are readily available online and it might be worth contacting your local council for some advice. Make sure your storage tanks are covered with lids, reclaimed materials or 'tarps' to prevent mosquito breeding and to reduce evaporation losses, algal growth and contamination.

Recycling water can also be done from household water waste like old baths and washing up bowls. However you recycle water, the environment and your plants will thank you for it – and so will your pocket!

It is important to provide your plants with sufficient water by keeping the soil around them moist at all times but not waterlogged. Always apply water in the cool of the morning or evening, when the wind is calm, to prevent water loss through heat evaporation.

BOOST YOUR MINDSET

Restore balance and stability with this simple exercise.

Stand with your feet hip-width apart, shoulders relaxed, and chin tilted slightly upwards. Picture a thread that travels through the top of your head and down your spine. Imagine that this thread is being tugged gently and feel your spine gradually lengthening.

Turn your attention to the soles of your feet and feel the weight of your body as it's balanced equally through each leg. Bounce lightly, bending at the knees and notice how you are supported by the earth.

Draw your hands, palms together, and pull them in to your heart. Close your eyes and picture a yin yang symbol in the centre of your chest. Focus on this image for a few minutes, and breathe deeply.

The yin yang symbol is universally associated with balance; this combined with a physical exercise that focuses on posture and movement helps to promote a sense of stability and equilibrium.

CINNAMON
Cinnamomum zeylanicum

Cinnamon trees are native to hot countries such as Sri Lanka and Malaysia. They grow to 9 m/30 ft in height, with brown, papery bark and shiny, tough green leaves. The flowers are creamy white and turn into blue, oval-shaped berries. Cinnamon trees thrive in a tropical climate with plenty of hot sunshine and rain, and a minimum temperature of 15°C/59°F. The commercial spice is made from the dried inner bark of young shoots. Trees are cut back close to the ground to encourage re-sprouting at low level to increase yield when harvesting.

This spice has been a vital medicine, incense and flavouring since Biblical times. In Indian Ayurvedic medicine it is considered an effective remedy for menstrual, respiratory, immune-system and digestive problems. The world's cinnamon trade was first monopolized by the Portuguese in the sixteenth century and was then taken over by the Dutch in the seventeenth century; it was a valuable commodity because of the popularity of the flavour.

PART OF PLANT USED Inner bark, leaves

ACTIVE INGREDIENTS Gum, mucilage, tannins, volatile oil

COMMERCIALLY AVAILABLE AS Whole, powdered spice, tablets, indigestion medicine, essential oil (from leaves)

ACTIONS Astringent, antifungal, antirheumatic, circulation stimulant, digestive tonic

USED TO TREAT

- INDIGESTION, GAS, SLUGGISH DIGESTION: tablets or indigestion formulae taken as directed ease gas in the bowel and stimulate digestive processes.
- COLDS, INFLUENZA, COUGHS: can support immune function; cinnamon-leaf essential oil can be used as a soothing inhalation.
- YEAST INFECTIONS (CANDIDA): two drops of essential oil added to a warm bathtub soothes irritation.
- RHEUMATISM, OSTEOARTHRITIS: Two drops of essential oil added to two teaspoons of sunflower oil, massaged into affected areas, improves circulation.

CULINARY USE As a spice in apple dishes, and in Middle Eastern and Indian savoury recipes.

SAFETY INFORMATION Whole spice is not to be used medicinally during pregnancy. Avoid using essential oil on sensitive skin, or on young children.

SOIL

To understand how to feed your plants, you need to understand your soil. We walk on it every day, we build on it, we dig it up, yet we often forget it is the most fundamental element in the garden. Soil looks relatively simple, brown and dirty, but it is full of life and is an incredibly dynamic and complex ecosystem.

SOIL: THE EARTH BENEATH OUR FEET

The soil consists of three layers: the topsoil, which contains the most nutrients and organic matter; the subsoil, where the partially decomposed rock exists; and the parent rock, which has a large influence on the nature of the soil and affects its pH and make-up.

SOIL MAKE-UP: SOIL PH

The pH determines which plants you can grow – for example, chalk soils are very alkaline and won't support plants like heather or rhododendrons, which prefer the acid soil found in clay, sedimentary rock soil. The pH scale is used by gardeners to identify their soils and what crops they can grow by measuring the acidity and alkalinity of soil ranging; the ideal pH reading for most plants to thrive in is 7.5.

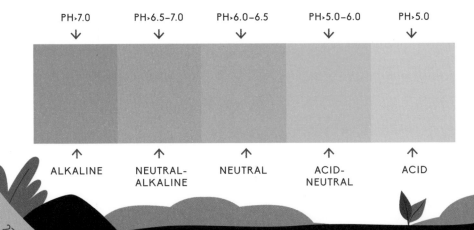

PH›7.0	PH›6.5–7.0	PH›6.0–6.5	PH›5.0–6.0	PH›5.0
↓	↓	↓	↓	↓
↑	↑	↑	↑	↑
ALKALINE	NEUTRAL-ALKALINE	NEUTRAL	ACID-NEUTRAL	ACID

SOIL TYPES

A soil's physical character is determined by the organic matter content and the balance of clay, silt and sand. This affects its workability, aeration and ability to retain or release moisture and nutrients.

CHALK Very alkaline and free draining but can dry out easily; although a fertile soil, the alkalinity prevents many of the nutrients from being made available to the plants. To combat this, regularly add well-rotted organic matter.

CLAY Clay soil is nutrient rich, but is heavy and difficult for air, water and plant roots to move through when wet; when dry it forms hard clots. To make it more workable, add well-rotted organic matter such as compost and manure.

LOAM Considered ideal for growing, loam is a mix of 40% sand, 40% silt and 20% clay, making a well-drained, moisture-retentive, nutrient-rich and easy-to-cultivate soil.

SANDY Sandy soils have large particles making them free draining, but leach water and nutrients, making them poor and prone to dry out. They are light and easy to cultivate and can be improved with the addition of well-rotted organic matter.

SILT Silt is soft and smooth and holds a lot of water, but is better draining than clay because the particles are bigger. It is found in river estuaries. Silt soil can become compact like clay and the addition of organic matter will aid aeration.

LUNAR GARDENING

Some gardeners believe the moon has a fundamental effect on the success of a garden. They are inspired by our ancestors, who watched the rhythms of the night skies and studied the relationship between the moon and plants and animals. Rudolf Steiner was an advocate of lunar gardening and suggested using the lunar and planetary influences to time activities such as sowing, weeding and harvesting. Sceptics believe lunar gardening is just ancient folklore, but there is scientific evidence to suggest it works. The Earth is in a large gravitational field, which is influenced by the moon and the sun. The moon pulls the tides and likewise has an effect on the soil water, causing it to rise and become available to plants.

During the New Moon phase, the lunar gravity pulls water up, making it a good time to sow seeds of plants that fruit above ground and annual crops that produce seed on the outside of their fruit.

In the First Quarter phase, the Earth is exhaling as the Moon's gravitational pull weakens, but the moonlight is strong. The sap rises and it is good for leaf growth and starting anything new.

WAXING MOON

NEW MOON

When there's a Full Moon, the moonlight is decreasing and the growing energy is pulled down towards the roots, making it a good time to sow root crops. As the energy is directed at the roots' top, regrowth won't be as rapid, so it's a perfect time to prune and weed.

As the moon wains, it is a barren phase where the plants need to rest and prepare for the next new moon. Gardening jobs for this phase are digging and mulching, mowing lawns to decrease growth and harvesting crops.

WANING MOON

FULL MOON

LET'S FERMENT SEEDS

Fermentation of seeds occurs as a natural process in the garden as the fruits fall to the ground and rot. Fermentation kills off any seed-borne diseases that can affect the next generation of plants. Only ferment seeds that you are likely to germinate in the short term, within five years. The fermentation process can easily be mimicked in the kitchen.

INGREDIENTS

- Spoon
- Sterilized jar
- Sieve
- Platé
- Airtight container

METHOD

1. Scoop out the seeds and pulp of your chosen fruit into a sterilized jar and fill it with double the amount of water.

2. Stir vigorously and store the mixture in a warm place at 30°C/86 degrees farenheit for up to three days until you see white bubbling on the surface of the mixture.

3. After a day of bubbling, pour the brew into a bowl of water and gently separate the seeds from the pulp with your fingers. Live seeds will sink to the bottom of the bowl.

4. Rinse and sieve the seeds several times, then place the seeds on a plate in a cool, dry place for several days before storing them in an airtight container.

5. Label the container with the type of seed and date. Store it somewhere dark and cool.

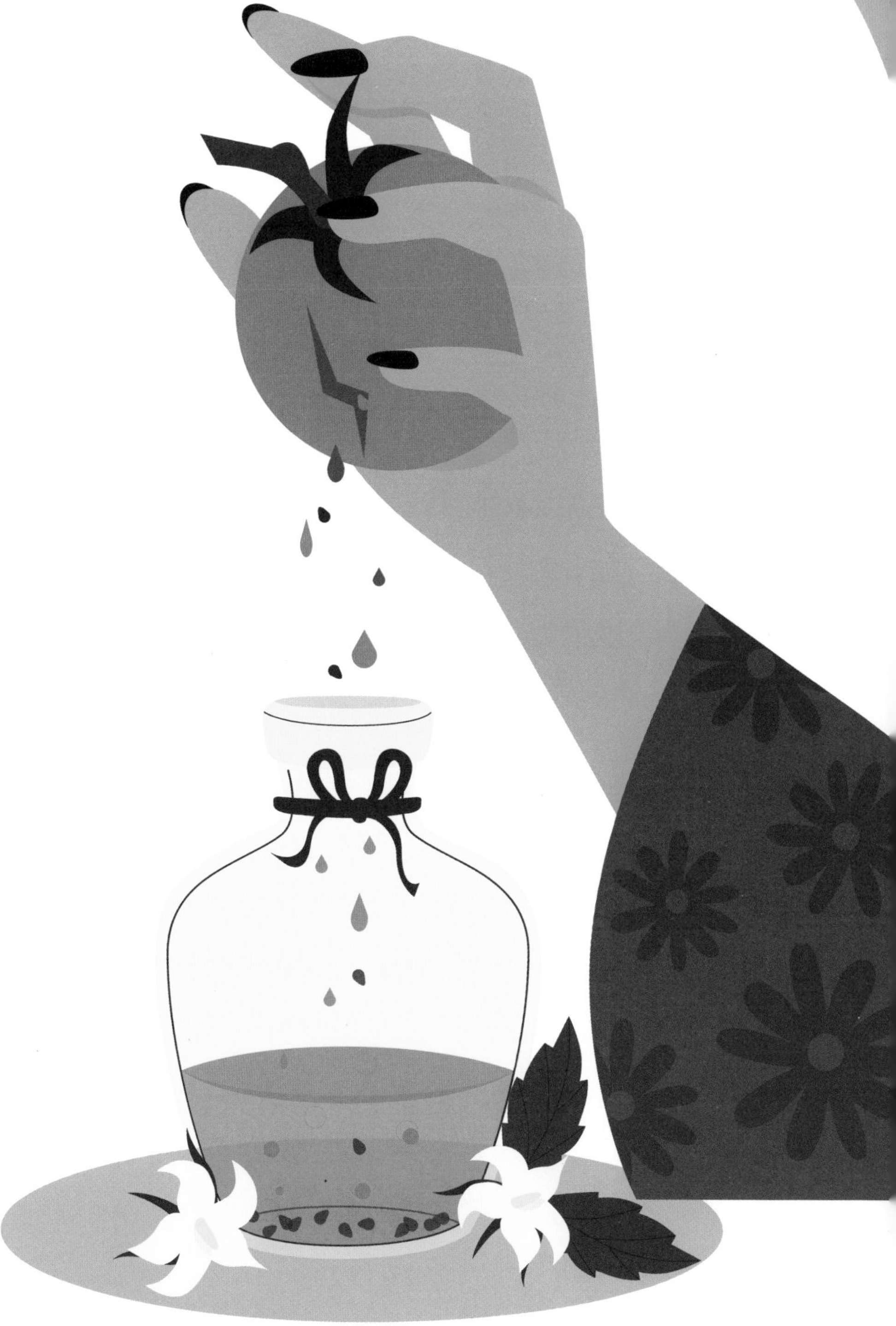

NATURE BY NIGHT

The night has special powers to free us from daytime worries.
No one will call or email you. People who give you stress are asleep –
in theory, at least. But how many of us lay awake at night, worrying
about everything and nothing; turning small problems into monsters?
To benefit from the calming effect of the night we need to turn off
the artificial lighting of our television and computer screens long
before we go to bed. In order to get into that wonderful state of
mind that the night can bring us, we have to go outside.

The stars; the moon; the silence; the darkness; it's all there for us.
With the absence of bright lights, your other senses fill in the gap. You'll
become aware of the soft touch of the night breeze on your skin. What
seems like silence turns into an orchestra of nature sounds if you pay
attention to it; high-pitched crickets chirping endlessly, night owls
calling, bats flying. What seems like darkness will turn into beautiful
shades of blue. If you take a deep breath, you smell the earthy aroma of
damp plants and trees.

ROOTS

Roots are a plant's primary way of gaining nourishment. Tiny hairs on the root reach out into the soil, using ion exchange to absorb nutrients. A plant that has been in the soil a long time has grown a great beard of hairy root filaments, not unlike the connections we form as members of a community. All those filaments and folds help connect a plant not only to nutrients in the soil, but also to other organisms around the plant. Through fungi in the soil, plants' roots of the same and different species can exchange nutrients and chemicals. When you pull up a root, many of these finer threads break off and remain in the soil to decay, adding organic matter.

In soils where nutrients are scarce, the roots' length can far exceed the height of the plant. These root structures help build the soil as well as the plant.

Roots not only suck up nutrients, they also act as the plant's cellar. In winter, plants store sugars, starches and nutrients in their roots whilst the rest of the plant goes dormant. For us gardeners, this translates as improved taste and nutrition in root vegetables, such as carrots and potatoes, which have been left in the soil through a frost or two. We crave root stews in autumn and winter because roots store well, but also because consuming a plant's roots gives us Earth medicine at a time when we seek the grounded stillness of winter. In traditional Chinese medicine, root vegetables are balanced and nourishing, neither too cleansing nor too rich. Many root vegetables are said to clear toxins, cleanse the blood and support digestion.

SHOOTING STARS

One of the most magical stargazing experiences we can have is seeing
a shooting star. They are always unexpected and totally unpredictable.
No wonder they give us that little feeling of thrill and wonder. They are
so fleeting, though, that by the time you see one out of the corner of your
eye, it's gone. If you are trying to spot one you need to be looking up with
a wide-open attention, and with your awareness on your peripheral
vision. This is actually quite calming, because when we feel safe, our
vision (and in fact all our senses) softens; when we feel anxious or fearful
and become hyper-vigilant our vision narrows.

A shooting star, or meteor, is created by a meteoroid (a small rocky
fragment of a comet or asteroid) searing through the Earth's atmosphere
and burning up. Meteoroids bombard the Earth all the time, mostly in the
form of dust or tiny sand grains. At certain times of the year you can see
a whole shower of them as the Earth passes through the dusty leftovers
of the tail of a long-forgotten comet. If the meteor is big enough to
survive the fiery journey downwards then it will hit the ground (or sea)
and we call it a meteorite.

A LEAPING HARE READING LIST

This almanac is made up of extracts from some of the best of Leaping Hare Press's books. To read more of the original writing, follow our reading list.

CONSCIOUS CRAFTS: 20 MINDFUL MAKES TO RECONNECT HEAD, HEART & HANDS

Conscious Crafts: Knitting
Vanessa Koranteng &
Sicgmone Kludje, 2022.

Conscious Crafts: Pottery
Lucy Davidson, 2021.

Conscious Crafts: Whittling
Barn the Spoon, 2022.

MINDFUL THOUGHTS

Mindful Thoughts for Artists:
Finding Flow & Creating Calm
Georgina Hooper, 2020.

Mindful Thoughts for Birdwatchers:
Finding Awareness in Nature
Adam Ford, 2018.

Mindful Thoughts for City Dwellers:
The Joy of Urban Living
Lucy Anna Scott, 2018.

Mindful thoughts for Cyclists:
Finding Balance on Two Wheels
Nick Moore, 2017.

Mindful Thoughts for Fathers: A
Journey of Loving-kindness
Ady Griffiths, 2020.

Mindful Thoughts for Gardeners:
Sowing Seeds of Awareness
Clea Danaan, 2018.

Mindful Thoughts at Home: Finding
Heart in the Home
Kate Peers, 2020.

Mindful Thoughts for Makers:
Connecting Head, Heart, Hands
Ellie Beck, 2019.

Mindful Thoughts for Mothers: A
Journey of Loving-awareness
Riga Forbes, 2019.

Mindful Thoughts for Runners:
Freedom on the Trail
Tessa Wardley, 2019.

Mindful Thoughts for Stargazers:
Find your Inner Universe
Mark Westmoquette, 2019.

Mindful Thoughts for Surfers:
Tuning in to the Tides
Sam Bleakley, 2020.

Mindful Thoughts for Walkers:
Footnotes on the Zen Path
Adam Ford, 2017.

OTHER CONSCIOUS LIVING TITLES

Book of Leaves: A Leaf-by-Leaf
Guide to Six Hundred of the
World's Great Trees
Allen J Coombes, 2015.

Gone: Stories of Extinction
Michael Blencowe, 2021.

Good Companions: The Mix & Match
Guide to Companion Planting
Josie Jeffrey, 2013.

Herbs: A Color Guide to Herbs and
Herbal Healing
Jennie Harding, 2009.

How To Plant A Tree: A simple
Celebration of Trees & Tree Planting
Daniel Butler & Simon Toomer,
2010.

Let's Plant & Grow Together: Your
Community Gardening Handbook
Ben Raskin, 2024 (forthcoming).

Let's Wildflower the World: Save,
Swap and Seedbomb to Rewild
our World
Josie Jeffery, 2022.

Silo: The Zero Waste Blueprint
Douglas McMaster, 2019.

Sleep Tight: Illustrated Bedtime
Stories & Meditations to Soothe you
to Sleep
Alison Davies, 2021.

The Domestic Alchemist: 501
Herbal Recipes for Home, Health &
Happiness
Pip Waller, 2015.

NATURE RESOURCES

'Nature is not a place to visit. It is home.' – *Gary Snyder*

BOOKS THAT ENLIGHTEN

Braiding Sweetgrass
Robin Wall Kimmerer, Penguin, 2020.

Enchantment
Katherine May, Ebury, 2023.

Losing Eden: Why Our Minds Need the Wild
Lucy Jones, Penguin, 2020.

Plant Magic: Herbalism in Real Life
Christine Buckley, Shambhala Publications, 2020.

The Almanac: A Seasonal Guide to 2023
Lia Leendertz, Gaia, 2022.

The Tree
John Fowles, Little, Brown and Company, 1979.

Why Women Grow
Alice Vincent, Canongate, 2023.

MAGAZINES & JOURNALS TO INSPIRE

Bloom

Ernest

Resurgence & Ecologist

Wonderground

SOUNDS TO TUNE INTO

BBC Radio 6 Music
Cerys Matthews

BBC Radio 3
The Great Chorus

Bon Iver

Kate Bush

Sigur Ros

POETRY TO CONNECT YOU

Daffodils
William Wordsworth, Broadview Press 2015.

The Peace of Wild Things And Other Poems
Wendell Berry, Penguin, 2018.

The Sun and Her Flowers
Rupi Kaur, Simon & Schuster, 2017.

INDEX

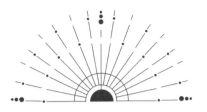

ABOUT RALU

Raluca Spatacean is a Romanian illustrator who is inspired by the balancing elements of wellbeing and the natural world. In 2013, she decided to follow her intuition and creative instincts to travel the world – living in Italy, Spain, Romania, Ireland and England–and experience living life with freedom and joy. In 2020 and throughout the global pandemic, she put pen to paper and discovered the joy of digital illustration, which she started to share with the world on Instagram, and soon found a dedicated community of followers soothed by her calming, positive artworks and writings.

@madebyralu

Leaping Hare Press

ABOUT LEAPING HARE PRESS

Leaping Hare Press creates beautiful books to inspire and empower readers to translate ethical and spiritual values into practical, meaningful life choices. Exploring nature, mindfulness, self-care and wellbeing, and penned by expert authors, our books present simple steps to help you to engage with each other and the natural world.

Thank you to all of our Leaping Hare Press authors – past, present and future – who together have created the heart and roots of the list.

If you liked this book then you may also like *The Leaping Hare Wellness Almanac: Your Yearlong Guide to Creating Positive Spiritual Habits*, published in 2022.